D1648577

Iniquity

Dr. Ana Méndez Ferrell

INIQUITY

....

Dr. Ana Méndez Ferrell

Iniquity
8th Edition, revised and enlarged 2011
© Ana Méndez Ferrell.

All Scripture quotations, unless otherwise indicated, have been taken from the King James Version and others.

Category: Deliverance

Published by: Voice of The Light Ministries
                     P. O. Box 3418
                     Ponte Vedra, Florida, 32004
                     USA

Printed in: United States of America

www.voiceofthelight.com

ISBN 13: 978-1-933163-36-9

Dedication

I dedicate this book to my beloved heavenly Father, to Jesus Christ, my Redeemer, and to the Holy Spirit. I also dedicate it to my beloved sisters, Mercedes Méndez, my twin, and Cecilia Pezet, and along with my nephews, Santiago and Pablo.

Content

Introduction

I am greatly weighed down within my soul as I observe thousands and hundreds of thousands of Christians suffering greatly, going through never-ending deserts, bearing sicknesses with no apparent relief and burdened by irrevocable curses. This suffering has caused me to intensely seek God's face in order to find a solution to so many unanswerable questions.

For many years, God has raised me as a pioneer in a number of areas, spiritual warfare being one of them at the personal and territorial deliverance level. As I have invaded these terrains and stood against the powers of darkness, I have realized that I need to comprehend God's righteousness in a deeper way.

The only force that destroys the power of the devil is the righteousness manifested on the cross of Calvary, which is much greater than the simple justification by grace preached in most churches.

Through this study, God wants us to discover the wonderful treasures hidden in Jesus Christ, so as to enter the fullness of life found in the depths of the mystery of the cross alone. God wants us to understand "iniquity" as the greatest obstacle to possessing the riches of His glory. Our ignorance about iniquity binds us to curses from which we cannot escape.

In His Word, God makes a specific distinction between sin and iniquity. The Church is used to dealing with the topic of sin to some degree, but almost never touches the vast problem of iniquity. Most Christians are unaware of its existence, so they are unable to be freed from it. Nevertheless, iniquity is one of the most significant topics in the Bible. Ignorance , and a lack of understanding about iniquity result in the greatest source of failure, oppression, and defeat that God's people face.

1

What is Iniquity?

Etymologically iniquity means "twisted and distorted." It is, in fact, anything that turns away from God's straight and perfect path. The origin of iniquity was found in the fall of Lucifer. It happened in the moment this archangel, full of beauty and perfection, allowed a thought that was out of line with God and started to believe in something different and opposite to Divine Justice.

Now, just as faith is the substance of what is believed, that is, the power that activates the invisible world of heavens, this twisted thought derived by the archangel produced a spiritual substance which was the origin of evil.

Thou wast perfect in thy ways from the day that thou wast created, till iniquity was found in thee. Thou hast defiled thy sanctuaries by the multitude of thine evilness, by the iniquity of thy traffick...

Ezekiel 28:15 and 18 (King James version)

The words iniquity and evil, are referenced numerous times in the Bible, and are fundamental to understanding the root of the vast majority of problems we suffer. Evil is the diabolic seed from which all wickedness originates. It is then transmitted to man in birth, impregnating his heart with thoughts and intentions opposed to righteousness, truth, love and everything God is. Iniquity is the sum of all twisted thoughts or the total of all that is evil in mankind.

Iniquity impregnates the spirit of the human being at the moment of conception. In that very instant all of the spiritual data or the spiritual inheritance of evil is established in the person. Iniquity operates as a "spiritual umbilical cord," that transmits the spiritual DNA of evil from one generation to the next. This is how the twisted, sinful legacy of man is imprinted and passed on to his children. These children in turn will twist it further by their own sins, and thus pass it as a baton of influence and consequences to the subsequent generation(s).

The sin of Judah is written with a pen of iron, and with the point of a diamond: it is graven upon the table of their heart, and upon the horns of your altars...

Jeremiah 17:1 (King James Version)

Iniquity is what the Bible calls the body of sin. As we continue our study, we will see how iniquity has formed part of the spiritual body within man, affecting his behavior, the structure of his thoughts and even the health of his physical body. The body of sin originates in the spirit and invades the soul and body, like mud that soils everything it touches.

Iniquity is intrinsically tied to the spiritual world of darkness, and it is there the devil binds us with the curses from our ancestors. It is in this place the legal bases of sickness are rooted and transmitted from the parents to their children and from the children to their grandchildren. It is also here where Satan's legal right is granted to rob, to destroy and even to kill us. Our iniquity will constantly prevent us from receiving the fullness of the blessings of God.

This is the main door that the devil uses to affect a human being's life, believer or unbeliever. It is through iniquity that the evil one permeates a man's heart in order to inflict all kinds of perverse, sinful desires. This is called lust. The inheritance of evil has been transmitted, and it is going to corrupt the soul so that it will desire to do wrong. It becomes an irresistible force compelling good people to commit abominable sins. This is why sons of alcoholics, after reaching a certain age, have an uncontrollable desire to drink. Some of them may be sons of Christians or pastors whom, without any apparent reason, begin to develop these sinful inclinations. The reason is that iniquity has not been uprooted.

But every man is tempted, when he is drawn away of his own lust, and enticed. Then when lust hath conceived, it bringeth forth sin: and sin, when it is finished, bringeth forth death.   James 1:14-15 *(King James Version)*

Not only does the devil interfere in man's life through iniquity, but this is where God will constantly manifest His judgments. Iniquity opposes divine justice by being a twisted form of it; therefore, a constant friction with God's righteousness will occur. Part of the essence of righteousness is that it judges all that opposes it. The purpose of God's judgments is to bring order to everything according to His will and His righteousness. Therefore, whenever paths in a person's life are twisted, judgment will come as a continuous divine action through trials, tribulations, deserts and others, so as to pull the person back to His divine order.

...for I the LORD thy God am a jealous God, visiting the iniquity of the fathers upon the children unto the third and fourth generation of them that hate me...
Exodus 20:5 (King James Version)

Please note that God is not talking to unbelievers, but to His own people. He is not visiting sin, but iniquity. Sin is just the fruit of iniquity. It is the superficial, visible part of something deeply rooted in the human being. Our sins are the branches of a large tree that grows stronger from generation to generation. Iniquity is the real root from which all evil inside us merges, and it is there that we must cut away.

Most believers confess their sins to God, but have never asked Him to blot out their iniquities. For this reason they continue suffering the terrible consequences of financial curses, incurable family sicknesses, divorces, accidents, and tragedies that would never occur with the protection of an omnipotent God.

As I said before, the fruit is not the same as the root, nor is the origin the same as when something has been given birth. Jesus not only came to defeat sin in our lives, but also to destroy all the works of the devil. When Moses cried out to see His glory, the Lord passed by before him and proclaimed:

And the LORD, The LORD God, merciful and gracious, longsuffering, and abundant in goodness and truth, keeping mercy for thousands, forgiving iniquity and transgression and sin, and that will by no means clear the guilty; visiting the iniquity of the fathers upon the children, and upon the children's children, unto the third and to the fourth generation.

Exodus 34:6-7

A principle we must understand as a source of great release in our life, is that God does not deal with evil in a generic manner. He is extremely specific, and so we must respond to the kingdom of darkness. One of the tremendous tragedies I see in the body of Christ is how people feel satisfied with general and simple prayers. Something like: "Lord, forgive all of my sins" or "Lord, forgive me for anything that I have done in the past" or perhaps "Lord, forgive me for all sexual sins." Although God hears the intention of our heart and forgives us as far as our eternal salvation is concerned, the legal bases in operation are unaffected with generic prayers.

God wants us to examine our hearts, as well as to understand evil and its consequences in the same dimension He does. He does not want the devil to have something to use against us. Jesus died for our complete deliverance, and every part of the cross and His Passion is related to the different areas where he paid the price for us, so that we might enter into a complete fulfillment in Him. We did not receive forgiveness for our sins alone. The cross also represents a comprehensive work in which each part of our spirit, soul and body are redeemed.

Surely he hath borne our griefs, and carried our sorrows: yet we did esteem him stricken, smitten of God, and afflicted. But he was wounded for our transgressions, he was bruised for our iniquities: the chastisement of our peace was upon him; and with his stripes we are healed. Yet it pleased the LORD to bruise him; he hath put him to grief: when thou shalt make his soul an offering for sin, he shall see his seed, he shall prolong his days, and the pleasure of the LORD shall prosper in his hand. He shall see of the travail of his soul, and shall be satisfied: by his knowledge shall my righteous servant justify many; for he shall bear their iniquities.

Isaiah 53:4-5, 10-11

In this passage of Isaiah, we see how His sacrifice on the cross touches several areas in which we must be set free and redeemed. A great part of the body of Christ restricts itself to receiving salvation from their sins, but live their lives overwhelmed with emotional and physical pain. They are trapped in prisons of the soul and the spirit, and above all, suffer the continuous burden of carrying their iniquity.

Jesus did a complete work so that we may live a life of fullness in Him. However, we will never see His total triumph in our lives if we do not understand how we have settled for less in our spirit, soul and physical being and how the victory of the cross applies to each one of these areas.

God differentiates between Iniquity and Sin

We clearly see that God differentiates between iniquity and sin in the ceremony of expiation described in the Old Testament, a type and shadow of what was to come for Jesus at Calvary:

And Aaron shall lay both his hands upon the head of the live goat, and confess over him all the iniquities of the children of Israel, and all their transgressions in all their sins, putting them upon the head of the goat, and shall send him away by the hand of a fit man into the wilderness.   *Leviticus 16:21*

Once again we see God specifically cleansing His people through a detailed confession of these three corrupt forms of the human condition.

Types of Iniquity

Voluntary Iniquity

This is the voluntary practice of evil and of someone fully cognizant and desirous to do evil.

Conscious Iniquity

This is the conscious evil in operation, which produces an inner struggle that leads to either falling into sin or practicing it. It is the root of all sins we have committed and which still tempts us.

On certain occasions the believer tries to follow God with all of his heart, but there is a hindrance he is conscious about. However, he does not know how to fight against it. At the very best he may be able to suppress it, but he knows that it may become a problem in the future.

Unconscious Iniquity

There is some Iniquity that comes from our past generations which is latent in our spiritual inheritance, and   is not easy to detect. This kind of iniquity is a time bomb that sooner or later may cause either a sudden downfall, or some sort of calamity. This is why we see God's servants who began their ministry with a great love towards the Lord, and then unexpectedly become involved in unspeakable sins.

Unconscious iniquity can be the cause of many problems, illnesses or disasters in a person's life. In some cases we attribute the problems to the devil's attacks or to some inexplicable causes. In order to detect this kind of iniquity, it is important to analyze as far back as possible what kind of sins and situations that our ancestors where involved in. It is also recommendable to pay close attention to our dreams and see how the culture we were raised in is rooted in our life.

1. Iniquity is part of man's spirit

A) Man is spirit, soul and body

The human being is like a living machinery, extremely complex and wonderful at the same time. A study of the systems and organs of our body will be enough to realize the amazing and detailed work of God. Of the three parts comprising our being, spirit, soul and body, the easiest to understand is the body, for it is visible and tangible. However, it has taken hundreds of years for medical science to decipher and understand it, and even now, there still remain many unsolved mysteries.

Man must be understood as a whole, combining the three parts that comprise him. Ignoring one of his parts will lead us into a mistake. That is why science cannot put the body and the spirit together, for they are totally ignorant about it.

As we know, the body is comprised of innumerable components so as to function properly. Likewise, the soul and the spirit are extremely complex invisible bodies we must know and understand in order to receive the victory Jesus won for us. Millions of Christians have failed due to the limited knowledge they have concerning the two fundamental parts of man.

Some theologies teach that the soul is comprised of the mind, will and emotions. Others say that the spirit consists of communion, intuition and conscience. Both beliefs are so deep that most people ignore them so as to not make life difficult for themselves. Unfortunately, this choice keeps millions of people bound to deserts and tribulations from which they cannot escape.

Others more versed in the study of these areas, in an attempt to explain believers' demonic oppression, have compared the triune man with the tabernacle of Moses. They allude to the body as the outer court, the soul as the "Holy Place" and the spirit as the "Holy of Holies", where God's presence dwelt in the Arc of the Covenant. Using this model, they explain how a Christian can be attacked or oppressed by demons in his body, and also how the spirits of sickness afflict the physical body.

They argue that the soul is the Holy Place, where Levites and priests entered. It is also accessible to demons such as fear, depression, wrath, etc., that are free to afflict it. They add that the spirit of man can only be possessed by God's Holy Spirit or the devil, but there is no mixing. Once stamped in his spirit by the Holy Spirit, he is absolutely pure, and, from that point on, the problem lies only in the soul and body. Although I share this theology, I believe God is taking us to a deeper investigation of the places in the spirit not yet revealed in the latter centuries. If it was done, it was not spread en masse. Considering the spirit as a combination of three parts only, communion, intuition and conscience, it would be the same as teaching that the human body is only the head, trunk and extremities.

Paul, in his first letter to the Corinthians, mentions that there is a natural body and a spiritual body (1 Corinthians 15:44). Both are made of a complexity of organs and systems connecting one another, and allowing one another to function in its own dimension.

The physical body in the material world, and the spiritual body is in the spiritual arena, even though they are linked together. Understanding this point makes me differ from the belief that the spirit is pure because God dwells there. Let me cite a few texts from the Bible to support my belief:

Having therefore these promises, dearly beloved, let us cleanse ourselves from all filthiness of the flesh and spirit, perfecting holiness in the fear of God.

2 Corinthians 7:1

And the very God of peace sanctify you wholly; and I pray God your whole spirit and soul and body be preserved blameless unto the coming of our Lord Jesus Christ.

1 Thessalonians 5:23

These verses contend that there is a spiritual contamination from which we must be cleansed, and God demands sanctification in all three parts of our being.

Without an exhaustive study of what the spirit is, which would take an entire book, let's observe our spirit's makeup and some of its different parts:

B) Parts of the Spirit

Communion

This part of our spirit is united with God through the seed of His Son implanted within us. This is the organ that determines if a spirit is alive or dead in relation to God.

This is one of the components in which God's voice is clearly heard and where He manifests His glorious intimacy which allows us to feel we are one with the Holy Spirit. It is in this area that the lordship of Jesus Christ is established, directing and reigning in our lives. This is also the place where the visions and revelations from the Spirit of God come to us, and where the Lord manifests in visible form to the ones who love Him and who have developed a life in the Spirit.

Communion is the central part of the spiritual body, and is the "Holy of Holies" of our temple. This place is possessed by the prince of darkness, whenever someone has not come to Christ. This is what the Word says regarding this topic:

To open their eyes, and to turn them from darkness to light, and from the power of Satan unto God, that they may receive forgiveness of sins, and inheritance

among them which are sanctified by faith that is in me.
Acts 26:18

Heaven and Earth converge in the spirit of man becoming one in Jesus Christ and setting His kingdom in our midst. It is through communion that we can see and penetrate the spiritual world and the hidden treasures of God, where we can experience His Glory and be transformed into His own image.

The life of God is conceived in this region, beginning with the new birth and eventually a new creature. Regeneration starts here, and makes us alive by the Spirit of resurrection.

Communion is connected to all other parts of our spirit, and functions as the governing place of our spiritual being, like the heart is the very marrow of the inner man. Communion is also the part that communicates man's spirit with his soul, specifically with his heart which is the store of his emotions and character. The Bible says:

Keep and guard your heart with all vigilance and above all that you guard, for out of it flow the springs of life.
Proverbs 4:23 (Amplified Bible)

Intuition

Although this word is not biblical, it is recognized by the dictionary and by some theologians as part of the spirit. Intuition represents the antennae connecting the natural world to the spiritual world. It makes us aware of a demonic presence, an angelic presence or a human spirit. It alerts us when we feel observed or followed for it is like a cosmic radar detecting the spiritual world around us, letting us know how things are with no logical explanation.

An example of this may be a strong feeling that we will receive a phone call providing us the answer we are waiting for. We can simply know a loved one far away is all right or, on the contrary, something is going wrong. In my experience organizing events for the ministry, I can sense formation of hindrances taking place in the spiritual realm trying to prevent the success of our planning. It is my spirit detecting what is happening in the invisible world and, as a result, I bow down on my knees and seek the Lord for an answer or directive.

Sometimes we know the results of an interview before it happens or, we detect someone has the intention of betraying us. Perhaps the words and actions of a person have the appearance of righteousness, but something in our spirit warns us about the danger. Through intuition, we receive revelation from God. Many prophetic words emanate from the ability of this part of our spirit to receive information about people. Gifts of the Holy Spirit such as words of knowledge, as well as, prophecy are manifested from this part of our spirit.

Conscience

This is the part of our spirit where the fear of God and the wisdom of God reside. It is the place where our being knows the difference between right and wrong without ever having read the Bible.

For when the Gentiles, which have not the law, do by nature the things contained in the law, these, having not the law, are a law unto themselves: Which shew the work of the law written in their hearts, their conscience also bearing witness, and their thoughts the mean while accusing or else excusing one another;) In the day when God shall judge the secrets of men by Jesus Christ according to my gospel.
Romans 2:14-16

Conscience, just as communion and other parts of the spirit, are intimately tied to the heart of man. This is why, on several occasions, the reasoning of the heart differs from that of the mind when it has not been renewed and it is conformed to this world. This part of the spirit awakened when man ate the fruit of the tree of knowledge of good and evil. When man continually sins, that part of God connected to his conscience, called the "fear of God", moves away from him. This causes the conscience to harden, becoming more insensitive to the will of God and ultimately producing thick veils that make their conscience to be seared.

Now the Spirit speaketh expressly, that in the latter times some shall depart from the faith, giving heed to seducing spirits, and doctrines of devils; Speaking lies in hypocrisy; having their conscience seared with a hot iron; Forbidding to marry, and commanding to abstain from meats, which God hath created to be received with thanksgiving of them which believe and know the truth.

1 Timothy 4:1, 2 and 3

The Mind of the Spirit

The mind of the spirit consists of various parts: understanding, spiritual intelligence and wisdom of God. The mind of the spirit is where the knowledge of God rests., It is where we supernaturally receive from Him knowledge that has never been taught by anyone. This is the part of our spirit that receives the mind of Christ, and illuminates us to understand something we could not understand before. This is the place where God reveals the great mysteries of science either to the righteous or the unjust. It is here where Paul prays for the eyes of their spiritual understanding to be opened for us to understand the riches of His glory.

That the God of our Lord Jesus Christ, the Father of glory, may give unto you the spirit of wisdom and revelation in the knowledge of him: The eyes of your understanding being enlightened; that ye may know what is the hope of his calling, and what the riches of the glory of his inheritance in the saints, And what is the exceeding greatness of his power to us-ward who believe, according to the working of his mighty power, Which he wrought in Christ, when he raised him from the dead, and set him at his own right hand in the heavenly places. Ephesians 1:17-20

In this scripture we can see different parts of our spirit. Paul is praying for them to be awakened and activated in us. We can see the knowledge of God penetrating our intuition, the eyes of our understanding bringing light to the mind of our spirit, and the area of our spiritual inheritance, which is the location of our spiritual genetics. We will discuss this later on. Another part of the spirit is the area of "The power of God" which receives the power of resurrection. It is in this part of the understanding where the light of God is established and where we may continue to grow in the light.

Spiritual Senses

Our body comprises of different senses that allow us to be in contact with the material world in a variety of forms. Likewise our spirit has different senses to perceive the invisible world. These senses help us to detect the origin of the things we perceive, either if it is from God or the darkness. This is what we know as spiritual discernment.

But strong meat belongeth to them that are of full age, even those who by reason of use have their senses exercised to discern both good and evil.

Hebrews 5:14

Every human spirit has got eyes, ears, taste, touch and smell. Visions and ecstasies are observed through our spiritual eyes. The voice of God, angels or demons is heard through our spiritual ears. We can also experience taste, just as John did in the book of Revelations, when he ate the little book he received from an angel which was sweet in his mouth and bitter in his stomach.

And I went unto the angel, and said unto him, Give me the little book. And he said unto me, Take it, and eat it up; and it shall make thy belly bitter, but it shall be in thy mouth sweet as honey. And I took the little book out of the angel's hand, and ate it up; and it was in my mouth sweet as honey: and as soon as I had eaten it, my belly was bitter.   *Revelation 10:9-10*

Spiritual touch is perhaps the most developed sense within us. It is the sensations of the Holy Spirit or the feeling of God embracing us. Many times during spiritual warfare, one can feel the spirit of death as coldness throughout their body even though the climate may be warm. Sometimes, a developed spirit will perceive spiritual fragrances, such as aromas coming from the presence of God, or the stench of unclean spirits. The senses of the spirit are connected to the senses of the soul, and compliment one another.

The Seat of Power

Our spirit possesses an area where the power of God resides. It is though this part of our spirit that the gifts of miracles, healing and wonders of God are manifested. It is like the engine of the spirit. It is the place where Samson received his strength. The same way this power came out of Moses' hand and later staff to depart the Red Sea. This is how we become the extension of God's hands.

As the prophet Habakkuk said:

And his brightness was as the light; he had horns coming

out of his hand: and there was the hiding of his power.
Habakkuk 3:4

Or, as Paul said:

Now unto him that is able to do exceeding abundantly above all that we ask or think, according to the power that worketh in us...   *Ephesians 3:20*

The apostles received the Spirit of God when Jesus blew on them before his ascension. However, He told them:

But ye shall receive power, after that the Holy Ghost is come upon you: and ye shall be witnesses unto me both in Jerusalem, and in all Judaea, and in Samaria, and unto the uttermost part of the earth.   *Acts 1:8*

This illustrates how the Holy Spirit can fill different areas of the spirit, activating them one by one, until arriving at spiritual fullness. That is why we observe believers in whom one part of their spirit is much more developed than others. Certain believers have developed a great intuition, or they move in the prophetic without any problems, but they are ineffective in the areas of power. The truth is that the gifts of the Spirit come through different parts of our being and develop in the corresponding area.

There is a principle that states: what it is done in

the natural realm is also done in the spiritual realm. Just as in our physical existence, we have natural gifts that are manifested in different areas of the soul and body, so it is with the spiritual body. Some people develop their mental gifts, in science, language and other professions. Many others are inclined towards the arts and sports; and, others develop a combination of them all.

Inheritance

Our material body stores genetic information in the chromosomes of the cell, which form a cord called DNA, where all of the data of our physical inheritance is kept. It is similar to a microchip in a computer, where all the information is stored.

DNA determines if we are born with features resembling our grandfather's eyes, mother's mouth, hair color of our great-grandfather, or the height of our father. All of this information is transmitted physically from generation to generation. When the cells of the embryo multiply within the mother's womb, a body is created and designed according to this information.

This same model is found in the spiritual body: a spiritual intangible DNA, where all the information proceeding from generation to generation is recorded with the name of INIQUITY. God provided us with a redeemed inheritance, founded in the Spirit of Christ, which must replace our cursed inheritance. Unfortunately, the Church continues suffering the consequences derived from this terrible part of the spirit, because it is ignorant about it.

Look how God Himself attributes the responsibility of man's own evil to his spirit:

For the LORD, the God of Israel, saith that he hateth putting away: for one covereth violence with his garment, saith the LORD of hosts: therefore take heed to your spirit, that ye deal not treacherously.   *Malachi 2:16*

Although this book does not pretend to make an exhaustive study in all the areas of the spirit, it is important to break them down, so that we may understand as much as possible, how this essential part of our being works.

I want to dedicate the following pages to the study of inheritance, so that we may obtain the wonderful freedom we have in Christ, and truly possess it.

2

The Conflict between the Two seeds

Iniquity is the Body of Sin

As we studied in the past chapter, iniquity is the evil seed conceived in the spirit of man, which is responsible for the sinful activity committed during his lifetime. The Bible talks about two seeds in conflict with one another:

And I will put enmity between thee and the woman, and between thy seed and her seed; it shall bruise thy head, and thou shalt bruise his heel.   *Genesis 3:15*

These seeds represent two natures, one demonic from the fall, and the other divine, through Jesus.

This is the seed of God's promise made to Abraham:

Now to Abraham and his seed were the promises made.
He saith not, And to seeds, as of many; but as of one, And
to thy seed, which is Christ.   *Galatians 3:16*

This divine seed is conceived in our spirit when we submit to Christ and accept what He did for us on the cross. From that moment on, an internal conflict exists between our "flesh" or "unrenowned soul" and the divine seed just planted in us. The flesh will be nourished with iniquity and will struggle to prevail. Whereas, the life of Christ will fight with the flesh, destroying it and empowering us to live by the Spirit.

What is flesh? This is the building the devil constructed in our soul using iniquity to turn our hearts from God's path. From birth, iniquity was implanted in our spirit and began to corrupt our heart, through reasoning, what we believe about ourselves, the way we develop ourselves, and even where we put our trust.

The flesh is, a complex structure. It is our internal upbringing as fallen beings, where all spiritual inheritance of iniquity was poured into us by the devil in order to accomplish his designs and not God's. The devil's function is turning us from the divine righteousness of God, by leading us to take our own fallen ways as a banner of behavior and self-justification.

Do ye indeed speak righteousness, O congregation? do ye judge uprightly, O ye sons of men? Yea, in heart ye work wickedness; ye weigh the violence of your hands in the earth.   *Psalm 58:1-2*

King David recognized this internal conflict that drew him towards evil, resulting in his falling into adultery with Bathsheba. He had a clear understanding of what had happened to him and prayed regarding the root of the problem.

Let's see how the light of the Most High clearly shows him the difference between iniquity, rebellion and sin. He understood that the reason for his sinful behavior was deeper than a simple sin, so he wrote :

Have mercy upon me, O God, according to thy lovingkindness: according unto the multitude of thy tender mercies blot out my transgressions. Wash me throughly from mine iniquity, and cleanse me from my sin. For I acknowledge my transgressions: and my sin is ever before me. Against thee, thee only, have I sinned, and done this evil in thy sight: that thou mightest be justified when thou speakest, and be clear when thou judgest. Behold, I was shapen in iniquity; and in sin did my mother conceive me. Behold, thou desirest truth in the inward parts: and in the hidden part thou shalt make me to know wisdom.   *Psalm 51:1-6*

Here we can see how iniquity is implanted at the very birth, and how it will constantly feed by the flesh, if it is not purged from our being, making us enemies of God, and invading us with death. These two seeds remain in conflict with one another until one of the two dies. If iniquity is not destroyed the consequences will be more than mere internal struggle, as we will see later on.

Iniquity springs from man's spirit and shapes the flesh with a certain structure, besides nourishing it with power. Iniquity manifests itself in the soul creating dense veils that prevent us from developing an effective spiritual life. It is the force that pulls us to live in our mind and heart, and makes us dependent on our own ways of thinking rather than God's.

The flesh, which, among other things, is the proof of iniquity being manifested in our life, is a concept so deep that we should consider more than its fruits.

Now the works of the flesh are manifest, which are these; Adultery, fornication, uncleanness, lasciviousness, Idolatry, witchcraft, hatred, variance, emulations, wrath, strife, seditions, heresies, Envyings, murders, drunkenness, revellings, and such like: of the which I tell you before, as I have also told you in time past, that they which do such things shall not inherit the kingdom of God.   Galatians 5:19-21

They are just fruit, the external evidence of a structure of habits and paradigms that have controlled our life for years and can be destroyed with the power of the Spirit alone.

Eliminating the fruit is merely an external change. A perfect example of this is an alcoholic who comes to Christ and stops drinking. Nevertheless, if he never confronts the roots of pain, bitterness, and rebellion that controlled him, inevitably, the power of iniquity behind his sin will draw him to other sinful behavior.

This is so, because his heart has recorded "You must escape. You can't handle the pain." What he has decreed over himself, is nourished by iniquity and will relentlessly pressure his flesh. As a result, he will eventually spiral down into a life of lies, adultery or cyber pornography, in order to avoid his pain. This person will believe he has been free from alcohol, but what he actually did was cut out an external fruit, rather than going to the root of the problem.

Pruning the superficial part or the visible sin is just an attempt at our sanctification, but it is not enough. This is why there is so much frustration, condemnation and hypocrisy in the Church. God wants to illuminate our understanding of these lines of iniquity so that we may obtain our true inheritance of abundant life purchased by Jesus.

As I've been intensely praying so as to find the way to take the church into its genuine life of glory and freedom, God revealed to me that very few of His people understand what walking in the Spirit means. This life does not consist of attending church every Sunday or even every day, either memorizing the Bible, or serving in a church. Walking in the Spirit has to do with how we develop each area of our spiritual being. It is a supernatural walk, totally led by the Spirit of God. It is the visible manifestation of Christ in our lives and the total destruction of the body of sin that, as we know, is called iniquity.

IT IS NOT MAN'S WILL WHICH DESTROYS THE WORKS OF THE FLESH; BUT THE SPIRIT OF GOD.

It is the seed of God destroying the demonic seed in the flesh. This is only accomplished by the understanding of the spiritual life and spending time in intimacy with God.

The flesh disguises itself in spirituality, ultimately attracting to itself horrible spirits of religiosity. Religion controls the flesh; it crushes it into a life of external habits and apparent devotion, but denies it the efficiencies of a life in Christ. Religion cannot deal with the internal part of our being, where iniquity lies, by means of rules and legalism. This is only achieved by the Spirit, when we adapt our spirit to God's Spirit.

Religious men enjoy DOING visibly pious things. However, that which is of the Spirit has nothing in common with doing, but with BEING. This is so relevant that if we do not understand it, we will be living according to the inheritance of iniquity in us, making efforts and sacrifices that accomplish nothing but making us tired of all that involves church. This is why we find many worn out servants of God, without strength and unsure what else to do or in which direction to go.

The devil's plan is to permeate the Holy Church of Jesus Christ with religiosity, so as to control it by iniquity, and thus, kill the life of the spirit.

We must understand that all that it is not born day after day in heaven and brought to us by the Holy Spirit, is born from the flesh and ends in death. Prayers may be done in the flesh as mental petitions full of weeping but lacking faith. The Bible may be read in the flesh with no revelation but only bounds to the letter. Faked worship may be offered to God as empty songs that come just from the mouth but without a genuine intention to reach Him. All of these things can be done with only the intention of carrying out the service, whereas the hearts of people are in their own thoughts. These are bounds of iniquity that dull the efficient development of the spirit.

In the vast majority of churches, there is little or no emphasis on worshipping in the depth of the Spirit, allowing the genuine flow of intimacy with God, so that believers may be empowered in their spiritual development.

There is a tendency to give priority to men's programs, instead of being led by the Spirit of God. This has produced a carnal Christianity (humanly structured) which lacks spiritual effectiveness in most members of a congregation.

It is relatively easy to create a religious system of rules and formulas that everyone can follow, because deep down in their hearts, many are afraid to enter the unknown and intangible ways of the Spirit, where they will not be able to control what is to happen, or explain it in a rational way. This is why it is easier to reject the things of the Spirit, which are incomprehensible to the common man, but rather manage the familiar.

Unfortunately, this attitude has invaded the church, making it ineffective, powerless and dead.

But God is knocking on the doors of our hearts once again, so that we may understand truths that will bring us to live in the fullness in Him by means of his knowledge and a spirit sworn in his power and wisdom. Like one who has truly crucified the flesh.

And they that are Christ's HAVE CRUCIFIED the flesh with the affections and lusts.   *Galatians 5:24*

The flesh is intimately tied to iniquity and serves the law of sin and death which is opposed to the life of the spirit. In several cases, it kills the spiritual life of the believer. In the letter to the Romans, we can see the struggle between the two seeds and how the outcome will determine our final destiny.

There is therefore now no condemnation to them which are in Christ Jesus, who walk not after the flesh, but after the Spirit. For the law of the Spirit of life in Christ Jesus hath made me free from the law of sin and death.
                                                  Romans 8:1-2

Note in this passage how God emphasizes that there is no condemnation for those who walk according to the Spirit. He does not say there is no condemnation for those who call Him, "Lord, Lord," because he is referring only to those who walk according to the spirit. Afterwards, the apostle mentions two laws which oppose one another: that of the Spirit of life governed by Christ through a spiritual life, and the law of sin and death, operated by the devil through iniquity.

As long as iniquity is not eradicated from the believer's life, he will continue to be imprisoned in the flesh. On one hand, he will attempt to live a spiritual life, because he loves Jesus; but he will be inevitably drawn to make carnal speculations that will lead him to make decisions according to his mind and emotions.

His opinion in spiritual matters will, most of the time, be influenced by corrupted religious thoughts, which will result in a slow development. He will be negative; and his faith will fluctuate. As iniquity always brings feelings of guilt, it will pressure the believer and fill him with fear and thoughts of death.

The objective of iniquity is to keep us focused on this world. It is the enemy of the cross and it will try to avoid it by any means.

As a ministry to the nations I have received several invitations from different countries to preach, However, I have been specifically forbidden to talk about the cross, or anything else that might disturb the comfort of the Church. Obviously, I have not accepted such invitations.

In many seminaries it is still taught that one should speak as little as possible about the cross and sin, in order to have a large church. Many ministers are trapped by iniquity having the appearance of spirituality, but seeking the fame OF THIS WORLD through large world ministries. They desire the recognition of great ministries and the favor of men. This is the reason why the preaching of the Word and the freedom of the Spirit are difficult because iniquity motivates the fear of man more than the fear of God.

Brethren, be followers together of me, and mark them which walk so as ye have us for an example. (For many walk, of whom I have told you often, and now tell you even weeping, that they are the enemies of the cross of Christ : Whose end is destruction , whose God is their belly , and whose glory is in their shame , who mind earthly things).   *Philippians 3:17-19*

The spiritual man is pleased when God is pleased. If it is a large ministry, great, and if it is not, that is good, too. The most important thing is to do the will of God, although it implies that we must lose everything here on earth so as to win everything in heaven.

For they that are after the flesh do mind the things of the flesh; but they that are after the Spirit the things of the Spirit. For to be carnally minded is death; but to be spiritually minded is life and peace. Because the carnal mind is enmity against God: for it is not subject to the law of God, neither indeed can be.   Romans 8:5-7

One thing clearly illustrated in the Scriptures is that one cannot BE from the Spirit and, at the same time, BE from the flesh. You are either one or the other. BEING from the Spirit implies a way of living and behaving with, objectives totally different from those of the world.

For some reason, the theory you can live in the flesh and in the spirit, for the righteousness of God no matter the way you live, has infiltrated the church. This is a big mistake, which has created, as a consequence, a Church filled with sin, sickness, religion and spiritual death. It is one which lacks implicit power in the victory of Jesus.

The Church does not have the slightest idea how to live by the Spirit. I believe God is calling us to stop and examine all of the doctrines that we have accepted , in the light of the results that they have produced.

3

The Dwellings of Iniquity

And the LORD God formed man from the dust of the
ground and breathed into his nostrils the breath of life,
and man became a living being. Now the LORD God had
planted a garden in the east, in Eden; and there He put
the man He had formed.   *Genesis 2:7-8*

God blessed them and said to them, "Be fruitful and
increase in number; fill the earth and subdue it. Rule
over the fish of the sea and the birds of the air and over
every living creature that moves on the ground."
                                        Genesis 1:28

Adam's soul was created to dwell in God, encased
in the Light of Christ, in a heavenly place called the
Garden of Eden. All of the knowledge, wisdom,

intelligence, counsel, power and the fear of God made up this spiritual place Through all these, he was able to rule over the Earth with the thinking and the mind of His Creator. This dwelling place was an unassailable fortress. That is to say, it was impossible for any kind of evil to penetrate it. It was God's own dwelling place with man.

Moreover, God gave Adam the "Free Will" as a tool to rule, and put the full possession of it in his hands. Nobody could use this tool but man alone. Neither God nor the devil.

Satan, then, decided to seduce the woman's mind, who used her free will to enter the devil's terrain. As a consequence, man lost his spiritual dwelling place "the Eden", his soul was separated from God and he lost his eternal life. His mind was reduced to 2% of its capacity and in a best-case scenario, a mere 10%.

The soul of man and his thoughts remained immersed in such a level of darkness and confusion that the only voice which would feed him was the devil's. From that moment on, the devil would be the only provider of all kinds of inferior, carnal, arrogant, sinful, limited and fearful thoughts, which would become the material over which the soul would build up its spiritual habitat. This is what the Bible calls "dwellings of wickedness" or "dwellings of iniquity."

For a day in thy courts is better than a thousand. I had rather be a doorkeeper in the house of my God, than to dwell in the tents of wickedness.   *Psalm 84:10*

The Earth is full of people who, literally, dwell in a spiritual and soulish place, totally opposed to the Eden. All these structures of Iniquity control, dominate, and affect them, and fill their societies and lives with evil.

Have respect unto the covenant: for the dark places of the earth are full of the habitations of cruelty.
                                        Psalm 74:20

After the fall of man, God stopped reigning over the Earth through His children and now it is the devil and death that reign through iniquity. The reflection of the Sheol thus becomes more visible by edifying in mankind all kinds of thoughts of death and fear that do not let them move forward.

Like sheep they are laid in the grave; death shall feed on them; and the upright shall have dominion over them in the morning; and their beauty shall consume in the grave from their dwelling.   *Psalm 49:14*

Iniquity molds our minds by creating strongholds that, literally, dictate our behavior. An example of this is the case of King Nebuchadnezzar. God judged his pride and iniquity. After which, he adopted an animal mentality. Man's behavior is a reflection of his spiritual dwelling place.

That they shall drive thee from men, and thy dwelling shall be with the beasts of the field, and they shall make thee to eat grass as oxen, and they shall wet thee with the dew of heaven, and seven times shall pass over thee, till thou know that the most High ruleth in the kingdom of men, and giveth it to whomsoever he will.

Daniel 4:25

Note in these passages how the spiritual world of darkness and death mold man's circumstances in the material world. These dwellings are spiritual, mental, or emotional structures from which we operate and from where we make decisions that do not come from God. Everything that is not built up in God is edified with iniquity, which is the substance of darkness. All of us have built up this type of dwelling around our souls.

A dwelling is, so to speak, an invisible mold that surrounds and shapes our soul, and gives it a personality and an identity. These structures are made by an aggregate of thoughts that dictate all that we are, and determine the fruit that we bear.

For as he thinketh in his heart, so is he: Eat and drink,

saith he to thee; but his heart is not with thee.

Proverbs 23:7

Man is the reflection of his soul's dwelling. A soul built up in God will think, act and bear fruit after God. The natural man or the Christian, who has not been spiritually edified, will think, act and bear the fruit of a limited mind structured by its culture and circumstances.

This structure, or dwelling of the soul, is the place of his security or insecurity; where he has settled on his own. It is a lie that it is built up in his inner man which dictates what he has to be. It is the place where all his limitations have been built. It is what makes a person think one way or another. These thought structures and emotions have been edified in his mind and heart since childhood, they are the result of iniquity. They are not undone merely because we say: "Lord, Lord, come into my heart".

These dwellings have to be undone by God's power, through our determination to topple them and through our faith in order to replace the lies with God's unlimited truth. It is not about repeating verses, but beginning to believe in a different way regarding ourselves. Seeing ourselves in the fullness of the greatness and power as God sees us, and acting coherently, leaves no rumor for any sort of doubt.

These are the most common structures:
- Dwellings of fear
- Dwellings of affliction
- Dwellings of illness
- Dwellings of scarcity and poverty
- Religious and Babylonian dwellings
- Cultural dwellings
- Dwellings of stress
- Dwellings of unbelief
- Dwellings of pride and egocentrism
- Dwellings of negligence
- Dwellings of addiction
- Dwellings of rejection
- Dwellings of destructive habits
- Dwellings of lust
- Dwellings complacency

Each one of the sins we have persisted in, will edify a dwelling. In order to knock them down, we must first recognize them, and define how they are controlling our lives. They not only rule our lives but also attract to themselves what they display.

For instance: someone can attend church their whole life and still live in dwellings of poverty, fear, illnesses, rejection, etc. These dwellings exert a power of attraction to all of these things, because the soul has been settled down and rooted in places of darkness where poverty, illness and rejection reign.

It does not matter how much that person proclaims with his mouth a Biblical truth. As long as his soul keeps established in those structures of thought, he will be cancelling God's power in his life and he will never overcome that area of his life. His inner dwelling becomes a tradition, a way of living, and a prison that does not allow him to see himself in a different way. This person has accepted a lie and he will live it until he decides to completely destroy it. Iniquity has formed a stronghold that needs to be demolished.

Making the word of God of none effect through your tradition, which ye have delivered: and many such like things do ye. And when he had called all the people unto him, he said unto them, Hearken unto me every one of you, and understand: There is nothing from without a man, that entering into him can defile him: but the things which come out of him, those are they that defile the man. Mark 7:13-15

What we have built up since childhood, our limited and traditional way of seeing and understanding the world, is what has corrupted us. Therefore, it is reflected in what we talk about and how we live.

This is why nowadays we have so many Christians who are sick, poor, oppressed, powerless, and dealing with deep character and sin issues. They have never destroyed the dwellings of iniquity in which their souls were formed. Besides, they have not established themselves in heavenly dwellings.

Many people relapse into their sins. They want to leave that lifestyle, and they do leave it for a while, but they never uproot the iniquity or destroy the dwelling that edified the sin in their soul.

We have the case of an alcoholic who fell into that slavery due to abuses he suffered in the past. His soul learned how to build up a structure using alcohol as a way to avoid or escape the pain. Later on, this man turns to the Lord and surrenders his alcoholism unto God's hands. He is delivered from the spirits of alcoholism but he never undid the structure of evasion. Sooner or later the devil will use this edification to lead him into new ways of evasion through another type of sin, such as pornography, verbal violence or whatever.

The same thing happens with poverty and scarcity. Throughout generations people have been internally edified with thoughts of poverty, inability and endless limitations. When they come to the Lord, they become Bible heads, some even become God's servants, but they never destroy those dwellings.

These dwellings are places of wickedness, that God did not build. People must leave them, otherwise, they will continue living with limited financial resources. Regardless of how much they sow in to God's Kingdom, they will never prosper so as to reach the measure God has prepared for them, since their souls are surrounded by structures that attract poverty to them.

With their mouth they confess God, but with their thoughts they make decisions according to their financial limitations. If they are going to build up a church, they picture it made of wood or inside a mechanic's shop. GOD DOES NOT THINK THAT WAY. Everything God thinks and plans for us, is magnificent.

I can only become that which is the essence of my spiritual dwelling: either God's dwelling or the dwelling places of iniquity.

The Church's main job is to edify God's dwelling place in each believer, not to fill us with Bible verses and formulas that deny the effectiveness of God's power.

And are built upon the foundation of the apostles and prophets, Jesus Christ himself being the chief corner stone; in whom all the building fitly framed together groweth unto a holy temple in the Lord: In whom ye also are builded together for an habitation of God through the Spirit. Ephesians 2:20-22

Jesus came to restore what had been lost. One of these things is, precisely, God's dwelling in the soul and spirit of man. King David entered the beauty and the power of those dwellings; but he could not settle himself, since this was only possible after the Holy Spirit descended on Pentecost. Nevertheless, the Father allowed him to enter God's dwelling, enjoy Him temporarily, and see His magnificence, which would be the inheritance of Jesus for us.

He that dwelleth in the secret place of the most High shall abide under the shadow of the Almighty. I will say of the LORD, He is my refuge and my fortress: my God; in him will I trust. Surely he shall deliver thee from the snare of the fowler, and from the noisome pestilence. He shall cover thee with his feathers, and under his wings shalt thou trust: his truth shall be thy shield and buckler. Thou shalt not be afraid for the terror by night; nor for the arrow that flieth by day; Nor for the pestilence that walketh in darkness; nor for the destruction that wasteth at noonday. A thousand shall fall at thy side, and ten thousand at thy right hand; but it shall not come nigh thee. Only with thine eyes shalt thou behold and see the reward of the wicked. Because thou hast made the LORD, which is my refuge, even the most High, thy habitation; There shall no evil befall thee, neither shall any plague come nigh thy dwelling. For he shall give his angels charge over thee, to keep thee in all thy ways. They shall bear thee up in their hands, lest thou dash thy foot against a stone. Thou shalt tread upon the lion and adder: the young lion and the dragon shalt thou trample under feet. Because he hath set his love upon me, therefore will I deliver him: I will set him on high, because he hath known my name. He shall call upon me, and I will answer him: I will be with him in trouble; I will deliver him, and honour him. With long life will I satisfy him, and shew him my salvation. Psalm 91

How wonderful are God's dwellings! They are totally opposed to the devil's dwellings, where people live full of insecurity, fear, lack illness, and are assailed by the fear of an unpredictable future and their human fragility.

God's dwellings are absolutely safe, impregnable, and full of health, abundance and the tranquility of a future designed and protected by God. However, God's dwellings are not built up in one second, simply because we repeat the sinner's prayer. We must build them up with materials from heaven, with gold, with silver, and precious stones that come from God's Holy Spirit.

He who has built his spiritual dwelling and has made it God's dwelling place shall live peacefully, in safety, in divine health, in the confidence that no sudden tragedy shall come upon him. He will be prosperous all the days of his life, because his soul prospers from the earthly realm to the spiritual one.

Knocking all dwellings of wickedness down depends, first of all, on subjecting our will to God's, so as to start effectively replacing lies with God's truth. First, I must now, not only believe, that no one can possess my free will, which is the most powerful tool to enter God's Kingdom and His inheritance.

THE BIGGEST LIE THAT THE DEVIL HAS MADE GOD'S PEOPLE BELIEVE, IS THAT HE CAN POSSESS MAN'S FREE WILL.

God granted man FREE WILL and no one, not even God or the devil can touch our will. God sealed it to become ours, for we will be judged for it.

The person who understands this will be truly free and will be able to grasp all the riches that Christ bought for us at the price of His blood. In Christ Jesus, I am and I have what I dare to be and to possess from His Kingdom. He has already given us all things pertaining to life and mercy. He has already given us the Kingdom, which means that the Kingdom is here and now, but only the violent take it.

My will joined to God's power is the instrument to knock down all the dwellings of wickedness that have ruled my life throughout the years.

By my own will, I decide to dedicate time and love to edify my inner self, and to meet up with Jesus in an unveiled face-to-face encounter, until I achieve the Kingdom in my life.

And I say unto you, Ask, and it shall be given you; seek, and ye shall find; knock, and it shall be opened unto you. Luke 11:9

Phrases such as: "The devil does not let me pray" or "I cannot do God's will because the devil doesn't allow me" are absolute lies. You are the master of your own will, and neither God nor the devil can force you to do anything.

You have in your free will, the power to make radical decisions that will lead to change. Some of them will require a fight, yet you and only you decide if you will fight with God to win or if you will surrender to the devil to lose. THE DECISION IS YOURS.

When Adam left God's dwelling, he found himself naked, and his alternate dwelling was to hide and to cover himself with vine leaves. God then asked him: Where are you?

God asks you the same question today. Where are you? What dwelling are you operating from? What is your life's condition? What are you producing in every aspect of your life? What is happening in your relationships with other people? In your health? In your finances? In your heavenly mission? When the world sees you, what do they see? Are the realities of heavenly truths being manifested in your life, or do you just live an alleged devotion to God, but your reality is full of limitations and dwellings that have been established in the defeated territory of the enemy?

God is calling us all to seek the true reality of the dwellings from where we operate. He is calling us to be aggressive against everything that is preventing us from entering the wonderful dimensions of His dwellings. He is calling us to leave the passivity and conformism of a Church that moves on mediocrity and which is not shaming the wisdom of this world.

We will stun and humiliate the mighty and the wise of this world when sickness does not touch us; when we do not have to borrow but we become the greatest givers of the world, when we become an incarnate example of God's love on this Earth, and when people from the lost world see the dwellings of God in each one of us.

4

The Operation and Manifestation of Iniquity

If we could visualize the body of iniquity, it would resemble a twisted black cord in our spirit. It is made of hundreds of thick knots, with layer over layer that appear to be filthy rags, filled with lots of information and covenants that have been accumulated from generation to generation. It resembles a tailback or a shell that constantly blocks or hinders life, preventing it to flow from our spirit to our hearts and, eventually, to our minds.

Iniquity produces Spiritual Deafness

Many people have their spiritual ears obstructed and are unable to hear God's voice due to the layers that iniquity has been knitting.

*The wicked are estranged from the womb: they go astray
as soon as they be born, speaking lies. Their poison is like
the poison of a serpent: they are like the deaf adder that
stoppeth her ear; Which will not hearken to the voice of
charmers, charming never so wisely.*

Psalm 58:3-5

God's plan is for each of us to hear His voice. This
is not just for prophets or for those who have the gift
of prophecy. The instructions from the Holy Spirit
depend upon our ability to hear God's voice. Entire
denominations are closed to this essential truth about
the Christian life; professing God no longer speaks to
us. Nothing is further from the truth. Jesus said, "My
sheep hear my voice... and they follow me." (John
10:27). When He spoke these words, the New
Testament had not even been written. He also taught
that the Holy Spirit would be sent to teach us all
things.

It is written in John 1:

*But ye have an anointing from the Holy One, and ye know
all things.*   *1 John 2:20 (NKJV)*

The anointing speaks to us and brings revelation
from God's word to our life. The Father designed the
spirit of man to be able to hear His voice. In fact,
every spirit is equipped to listen to the different

voices that come from the spiritual world. You will agree everyone has heard the devil's voice. We have all heard voices of fear, anxiety, discouragement, negativism, etc. This clearly demonstrates our capacity to hear the spiritual world. One of the greatest lies from the devil is that we are unable to hear God's voice. What kind of father would God be to have designed his family to hear only the devil's voice and not His?

In fact, if we open our understanding a little, we will realize that God has always spoken to us. That impulse preventing you from crossing the street saved you from being knocked down. Or, something in your heart that told you not to get closer to someone who had wrong intentions towards you, and you changed your direction. Or, that sweet voice who told you: come to your wife and ask her for forgiveness, and the problem was solved. God's voice becomes clear and it is not obstructed according to the level of iniquity present in our lives.

Behold, the LORD's hand is not shortened, that it cannot save; neither his ear heavy, that it cannot hear: But your iniquities have separated between you and your God, and your sins have hid his face from you, that he will not hear.   Isaiah 59:1-2

Note that the passage says iniquities. There are

areas where someone has been deeply treated by God, in a specific direction and is able to hear clearly. But there are other areas in continuous conflict, and the person does not know how to solve the problem. This occurs where the understanding has been dulled; a cumulus of iniquity has obstructed the spiritual ear.

Iniquity can be found in specific areas of our lives. For instance, a minister may hear clearly what God desires for the church he serves, but he may have difficulties finding God's will concerning financial matters. This could be the result of his past or ancestors, in which sinful activity in the financial arena occurred. Perhaps fraudulent business was conducted harming innocent people, maybe a robbery, an unpaid debt or lack of integrity. As long as this is not confessed as sin and iniquity, it will create blockage in the spiritual ear, as well as attract problems in finances. It is extremely important to make a detailed analysis of our works and those of our ancestors in order to identify our iniquity and to uproot it completely from our life. Of course, this is impossible without the revelation of the Holy Spirit.

We must go to Him and ask Him to help us eliminate all iniquity from our being. We must also ask Him to show us, by means of dreams or a gift of knowledge, where iniquity is rooted in specific areas of our lives.

Sometimes, our spiritual ear is so obstructed that we need the help of a minister of God to assist us to define the areas of iniquity in us. It is easy to fall into spiritual laziness and carelessness, and take an attitude that makes us think "Let others hear for me, because I do not hear a thing." This is iniquity in action.

This can also happen in other areas of our soul, such as our emotions. There are people who have constant conflicts regarding this area, and are unable to hear God's voice to solve them. It is very common in the case of people who often have sexual dreams and aberrations. They pray and ask the Lord to forgive their dreams or their fantasies, but the problem never comes to an end. The reason is they have not confessed their iniquity.

The vast majority of people make general confessions, such as, "Lord, forgive all sexual sin that I or my ancestors have committed." Unfortunately, this does not help very much. It might be enough in the case of a deathbed confession, but it is not enough for the rest of us.

In the spiritual world, every sin grows from a root of iniquity, and it has been recorded. It is very important to make a detailed list, assisted by the Holy Spirit, and ask forgiveness for each one of our actions.

There are people who fill an entire notebook, recording one by one all of their sins. But, believe me, if you take the time to do this, you will be totally free and live a life of peace. This is important for married couples, whose lives are riddled with guilt from sexual dreams and fantasies, frequently undermining their sex life. Dear reader, God has not forsaken you, but iniquity is a hindrance greater than what you may realize.

Iniquity produces Spiritual Blindness

As God designed us to have spiritual hearing, He gave us spiritual eyes. These are the eyes of understanding, which permit us to see with clarity God's truths and to behold His glory. Can we all see in the spiritual world? Of course we can, but we cannot operate in the truth unless we understand it and believe it for our life, first.

Before our personal encounter with Christ, we did not know we could heal the sick or cast out demons in His name. Perhaps, we were taught it could be done in biblical times, but not today.

In my case, when I read the Word: "These signs would follow those who believed in Jesus", I fully believed in this Word, which became alive in my life. The same thing happened when I realized we could see the kingdom of God, and that this ability was not just for a few people, but for everyone who turned to God with all their heart.

Nevertheless when it shall turn to the Lord, the vail shall be taken away. Now the Lord is that Spirit: and where the Spirit of the Lord is, there is liberty. But we all, with open face beholding as in a glass the glory of the Lord, are changed into the same image from glory to glory, even as by the Spirit of the Lord.   2 Corinthians 3:16-18

Here, we can clearly see that when the Spirit of God is present, he allows us to see as in the glass, His glory. This is a reality that thousands of people are living. The question is: why can't all people see it? There are two main reasons. The first one is veils of iniquity that have not been removed neither from understanding, nor from their spiritual senses. The second one, for those mature in the Lord, is from not developing their spiritual vision. Some have never believed it was possible, and have thought it not important. Others have not given emphasis to spiritual vision, in comparison to other gifts.

Let's focus on the first great cause: the veils of iniquity. The apostle Paul points out that the work of the devil is focused on producing spiritual blindness.

In whom the god of this world hath blinded the minds

of them which believe not, lest the light of the glorious gospel of Christ, who is the image of God, should shine unto them.   *2 Corinthians 4:4*

He also says:

In fact, their minds were grown hard and calloused [they had become dull and had lost the power of understanding]; for until this present day, when the Old Testament (the old covenant) is being read, that same veil still lies [on their hearts], not being lifted [to reveal] that in Christ it is made void and done away. Yes, down to this [very] day whenever Moses is read, a veil lies upon their minds and hearts. But whenever a person turns [in repentance] to the Lord, the veil is stripped off and taken away.
                        2 Corinthians 3:14-16 (Amplified Bible)

Now then, even though the apostle is referring to those who have never approached Christ, he is also speaking of those who are skeptics. Thousands of Christians have believed in Jesus as their Savior, but in many areas of their lives they are skeptical.

The reason is their hearts are still corrupted with iniquity, which has not been purged. This has formed veils of varying intensities producing spiritual blindness. In order to remove them, it is necessary to identify the areas of our heart that have not yet been surrendered to the lordship of Christ. When these areas are converted to Him, the veils will be removed.

Only the presence of the Holy Spirit can transform our hearts, He is the One who sets the captives of the heart and mind free from the prisons of darkness. This is why it is important to spend time with the Lord, for in the measure he brings His glory to our lives, we can see His light that changes us into His image. Christ is the image of the invisible God, and it is His image in us that beholds with open face the glory of God.

Jesus said:

Yet a little while, and the world seeth me no more; but ye see me: because I live, ye shall live also.

John 14:19

He also taught, saying:

As thou hast sent me into the world, even so have I also sent them into the world.   *John 17:18*

Jesus was sent, full of the Holy Spirit and the ability to see and hear everything that the Father was doing. Likewise, He sends us, to see and hear what He does.

Then answered Jesus and said unto them, Verily, verily, I say unto you, The Son can do nothing of himself, but what he seeth the Father do: for what things soever he doeth, these also doeth the Son likewise. For the Father loveth the Son, and sheweth him all things that himself doeth: and he will shew him greater works than these, that ye may marvel.   John 5:19-20

The majority of God's children do not move in this freedom. Iniquity fills them with unbelief or guilt, and the truth is that the devil has used the veils of darkness to make the Church blind. His objective is for the Church to be powerless to move in the fullness of what Jesus has bought with His blood.

Seeing the kingdom of God and beholding His glory is the most wonderful thing that could ever happen to us. It is worth doing whatever is necessary to obtain it. That is to say, to cleanse iniquity from our hearts.

Iniquity produces Sickness and Pain

Iniquity is the principle cause of sickness. Although it has its origin in the spirit of man, it travels through the soul and manifests physically destroying the body.

Science recognizes it as psychosomatic illnesses. According to the doctors, this type of disease originates in the mind, and produces chemical reactions in the organs that make the individual end up mined. This is in a large part a response of our body to feelings of hatred, bitterness, resentment, shame, etc.

This is actually much more complex than a mere chemical reaction. It is a spiritual matter. Iniquity that has been carried generation after generation has entered so deep in the lives of people, that it affects the genetics or heritage of their physical bodies. We are born with this iniquity, which intensifies as we contaminate our hearts with all kinds of sin and perversity.

We have already observed, how the spirit, soul, and body are intimately intertwined, and how the condition of the first two will determine how the condition of the entire body is affected. The apostle John says in his third epistle:

Beloved, I wish above all things that thou mayest prosper and be in health, even as thy soul prospereth.

3 John 1:2

A spirit filled with the presence of God along with a pure heart, purged and free from iniquity, will result in a healthy body, or the health of the "Kingdom." The opposite is a body in pain and prone to sicknesses.

Psalms 109:18 talks about the heathen man or the iniquitous, saying:

As he clothed himself with cursing like as with his garment, so let it come into his bowels like water, and like oil into his bones.   *Psalm 109:18*

Iniquity forms a type of thick toxic liquid, which accumulates in a body, deteriorating the organs and one's general state of health. Iniquity also resides inside the bones, weakening them and affecting the blood's quality. Let us remember that life is found in the blood according to the Bible and it is in the bone marrow, where blood is produced. All illnesses in the blood such as diabetes, leukemia, high or low blood pressure, lupus, etc., originate from iniquity.

Another example would be sadness which does not come from the Lord, and which causes death (2 Corinthians 7:10b). Death will cling to iniquity and will penetrate the bones.

Have mercy upon me, O LORD, for I am in trouble: mine eye is consumed with grief, yea, my soul and my belly. For my life is spent with grief, and my years with sighing: my strength faileth because of mine iniquity, and my bones are consumed.   *Psalm 31:9-10*

Sickness residing in the bones and joints, such as

osteoporosis, arthritis and rheumatic pain are the result of continual impregnation of this secretion that comes from iniquity. The formation of tumors and sharp muscular pain can be the result of physical body's reaction to this spiritual inheritance.

None calleth for justice, nor any pleadeth for truth: they trust in vanity, and speak lies; they conceive mischief, and bring forth iniquity. They hatch cockatrice' eggs, and weave the spider's web: he that eateth of their eggs dieth, and that which is crushed breaketh out into a viper.   Isaiah 59:4-5

Many times, when we have cast out demons, the Lord has shown us the way iniquity penetrates the body in the shape of eggs, forming tumors or cancers that spread and multiply throughout other organs (metastasis). Dense darkness manifested like a spider's web starts to interweave in the muscles originating strong pains and physical weakness.

Iniquity is against the body

Iniquity, as we have already seen, originates in the spirit of man, and passes to his soul building his structures of behavior. Finally, this passes to the body making it sick and destroying its functions.

Let us remember that iniquity is like a message

distorted gradually from generation to generation. Therefore, all destructive habits against the human body are related to iniquity. Vices and disturbances may come from our past generations or may be developed for ourselves. For instance, if a grandfather was a smoker, then, the father will be a smoker but also an alcoholic, and the son adds to these vices marijuana, whereas the grandson consumes cocaine and crack in his early years.

This is like a chain which continues distorting until someone breaks it and redeems the generational line with the blood of Christ, cleansing the bloodline from iniquity. It is important to remember that, where the fathers do not recognize the cause of the problem in their sons, they will never have the power and authority to help them.

Another example of iniquity against the body is the medicine consumption. Nowadays, pharmacological drug consumption is socially accepted. The Church, for instance, is not against medication, therefore most of its members consume several kinds of medicines that have not necessarily been diagnosed by a doctor.

The question is: where does this practice come from? The allopathic medicine consumed nowadays, began in the alchemy of the Middle Ages. In Greek, its name was "Pharmakeia" and it was ruled by the gods Asclepius (Greek name) or Asklepio (Roman name) and Hygeia, whose symbols are represented in the Medical Science (a short staff entwined by two serpents). The Word "Pharmakeia" is used in the Bible to describe witchcraft, which is also used for drug addiction, nicotine poisoning, alcoholism, and medicine consumption.

Jesus Christ carried our illnesses on the cross the same than we did our sin and iniquity. Therefore, the truly Christian should walk towards freedom from medicines.

Maturity in Christ drives us to depend entirely on His redemptive work. On the other hand, medicine does not have power to heal, and this is very well known by doctors and pharmaceutical companies. Medicine, just like witchery, may reduce temporarily an illness, but inevitably it will bring another. Only God heals.

It is not my intention to condemn anybody who thinks he has to take medicines, rather to show them a better way. I have seen parents tied to medicine praying for their sons who are immersed in drug consumption. I am not surprised that they do not see good results. Their sons are escaping from an emotional suffering through drugs, whereas they solve their physical and emotional problems by consuming medicines.

Being bound to "Pharmakeia" is a type of iniquity that mines the cells of the body and makes the immunological system useless. On the other hand, most of us do not know what those attractive pills with fascinating and trustful names prescribed by doctors, are made of. Do you know the truly destructive power of medicine? Why are there secondary affects produced that we prefer to ignore?

If we are really committed to Jesus Christ so as to depend on the healing power of His Holy Spirit who dwells inside of us, do you not think that we will see better results without secondary effects? I am not only saying IT WORKS, but you will also have the authority to defeat what is affecting your own health and the health of the ones you love.

Iniquity is also manifested in the body through eating disorders. There are people who eat excessively, ignoring that they are committing sin against their own body and destroying the dwelling of the Holy Spirit.

In the United States, for instance, there are about four million people weighing more than 300 pounds, and another four hundred thousand people are above

400 pounds. Iniquity makes people eat immeasurably. This is a root of self-destruction, maybe generational, that must be uprooted in order to reach freedom in this area. Therefore, it is important to recognize gluttony as iniquity. This offends God and brings terrible consequences to our body.

Maybe someone among your ancestors destroyed his body through suicide, nicotine poisoning or drugs, and iniquity is manifesting in your life destroying your body through food.

Iniquity and the Captivity of the Soul

As we have previously studied, iniquity manifests in the body as black water and oil that make the body sick. However, the origin of these substances is in the spirit of man. Iniquity in the invisible world of the human being will affect his whole physical environment. It is like a fountain that flows from his inner being, creating dense spiritual swamps where the soul of a person gets stuck, or even a righteous person sinks in a cesspit without exit.

Let us see what the word says:

But the wicked are like the troubled sea, when it cannot rest, whose waters cast up mire and dirt.

Isaiah 57:20

Note in this next verse how the righteous are trapped by collective iniquity:

For our transgressions are multiplied before thee, and our sins testify against us: for our transgressions are with us; and as for our iniquities, we know them; In transgressing and lying against the LORD, and departing away from our God, speaking oppression and revolt, conceiving and uttering from the heart words of falsehood. And judgment is turned away backward, and justice standeth afar off: for truth is fallen in the street, and equity cannot enter. Yea, truth faileth; and he that departeth from evil maketh himself a prey: and the LORD saw it, and it displeased him that there was no judgment.

Isaiah 59:12-15

Spiritually, all this mud of iniquity is cast upon others through violent perverse words, threats, slander, unjust accusations and pressures of all kinds. Nowadays, many stressing situations come from iniquity that has been accumulated until the individual literally feels he is suffocated. These people have controlling spirits, which oppress, castrate, and manipulate them, polluting the places where they reside.

Psychological problems such as fears or claustrophobia, originate from this type of spiritual environment. Many times, even though the conditions have changed, the soul remains captive in the past and deliverance becomes necessary. Being surrounded by these waters may generate fear, nightmares, affliction of spirit and great desperation. Many times, King David found himself surrounded by these muddy waters that literally were drowning him.

Because of the voice of the enemy, because of the oppression of the wicked: for they cast iniquity upon me, and in wrath they hate me. My heart is sore pained within me: and the terrors of death are fallen upon me. Fearfulness and trembling are come upon me, and horror hath overwhelmed me.   Psalm 55:3-5

This mud is real in the spiritual world. It causes a person to feel as though they are standing in quick sand. Only the power of God is enough to escape. These situations are frustrating because there appears to be no way out, nothing to hold, and the more we struggle the more we sink.

Save me, O God; for the waters are come in unto my soul. I sink in deep mire, where there is no standing: I am come into deep waters, where the floods overflow me. I am weary of my crying: my throat is dried: mine eyes fail while I wait for my God. They that hate me without a cause, are more than the hairs of mine head: they that would destroy me, being mine enemies wrongfully, are mighty: then I restored that which I took not away.
Psalm 69:1-4

We find this condition in the soul of the psalmist, who has been harassed by evil. Iniquity has been cast upon him and his soul has entered into captivity:

For my soul is full of troubles: and my life draweth nigh unto the grave... Thou hast laid me in the lowest pit, in darkness, in the deeps... I am shut up, and I cannot come forth.   Psalm 88:3, 6-8b

When we have been blessed with the ability to see the spiritual world, we can witness how these pits are literally, places where the devil has imprisoned a part of the soul, releasing all kinds of oppression and calamity. The soul is fragmented and held captive as a result of iniquity, traumas or evil harassment.

King David cried out to God in situations like this when he was terribly oppressed by the iniquity of his enemies:

The sorrows of death compassed me, and the floods of ungodly men made me afraid. The sorrows of hell compassed me about: the snares of death prevented me.   Psalm 18:4-5

He also says:
For without cause have they hid for me their net in a pit, which without cause they have digged for my soul.
                                                    Psalm 35:7

Job also speaks of these holes dug for the soul:
Yea, ye overwhelm the fatherless, and ye dig a pit for your friend.   *Job 6:27*

These prisons of darkness are not only produced by people that cast iniquity, hatred and curses over us, but we may be trapped in those places of great affliction because of our own responsibility.

Such as sit in darkness and in the shadow of death, being bound in affliction and iron; Because they rebelled against the words of God, and contemned the counsel of the most High...Fools because of their transgression, and because of their iniquities, are afflicted. Their soul abhorreth all manner of meat; and they draw near unto the gates of death.   *Psalm 107:10-11 and 17-18*

Those who do not give the glory to God are also trapped in these places:

Hear ye, and give ear; be not proud: for the LORD hath spoken. Give glory to the LORD your God, before he cause darkness, and before your feet stumble upon the dark mountains, and, while ye look for light, he turn it into the shadow of death, and make it gross darkness. But if ye will not hear it, my soul shall weep in secret places for your pride; and mine eye shall weep sore, and run down with tears, because the LORD' flock is carried away captive.   *Jeremiah 13:15-17*

We must follow the direction of the Holy Spirit if we are to rescue souls from these pits. We must have permission from God to set these people free and ask Him to show us by the Spirit the cause of their captivity and how the situation originated. Then, it is necessary to ask forgiveness for sin, iniquity, or rebellion. It is necessary to forgive those responsible for the harm, and finally, command that part of the soul to "BE SET FREE." And, to those who dwell in regions of darkness, we must tell them "TO LEAVE THE DARKNESS AND COME INTO THE LIGHT."

Thus saith the LORD, In an acceptable time have I heard thee, and in a day of salvation have I helped thee: and I will preserve thee, and give thee for a covenant of the people, to establish the earth, to cause to inherit the desolate heritages; That thou mayest say to the prisoners, Go forth; to them that are in darkness, Shew yourselves. They shall feed in the ways, and their pastures shall be in all high places.   Isaiah 49:8-9

Sometimes, it has been necessary in the natural world to hold certain people by the hand and remove them from the hole. Spiritually, the deliverer as well the one being set free may experience a sensation of victory and liberty. Then, we must ask God to place this soul in heavenly places in order to be nurtured by the Holy Spirit. The results obtained after deliverance such as this are wonderful (I recommend reading my book "Regions of Captivity"[1] where I go deeper into this topic).

Iniquity and the Torrents of Perversity

As we observed in the last paragraph, iniquity manifests in the spiritual world as miry clays that are cast over someone, just or unjust, causing, most of the times, great oppression.

Attend unto me, and hear me: I mourn in my complaint, and make a noise; Because of the voice of the enemy, because of the oppression of the wicked: for they cast iniquity upon me, and in wrath they hate me. My heart is sore pained within me: and the terrors of death are fallen upon me.   Psalms 55:2-4

These muds eventually become spiritual swamps or torrents of perversity sent by the devil to devastate a person and make him sink in the circumstance. In certain occasions, King David found himself surrounded by these miry waters that were literally drowning him.

Save me, O God; for the waters are come in unto my soul. I sink in deep mire, where there is no standing: I am come into deep waters, where the floods overflow me. I am weary of my crying: my throat is dried: mine eyes fail while I wait for my God. They that hate me without a cause, are more than the hairs of mine head: they that would destroy me, being mine enemies wrongfully, are mighty: then I restored that which I took not away.

Palms 69: 1-4

This miry clay is real in the spiritual world, and creates pits from which we cannot escape without the help of the Lord. This is manifested in the natural through situations in which we feel desperate and it seems to us there is no escape. We are unable to find a place to stand. The more we try to leave, the deeper we go. People with huge debts are in these swamps, as well as those who are entangled in businesses that end up in a demand or judgment that threatens to destroy them completely. Most of these people tend to lie and are easy prey and become more and more entangled, drowning in a torrent of perversity.

These torrents are also manifested when the devil sends slanders to destroy someone completely. King David cries out to God in a similar situation, where he is terribly oppressed by the iniquity of his enemies:

The ropes of death entangled me; floods of destruction (iniquity) swept over me. The grave wrapped its ropes around me; death laid a trap in my path.

Psalm 18:4-5 (New Living Translation)

In this scripture we can see how a river of threats

and strategies of death rise to make King David a pray of terror. This is what we see when someone righteous finds himself trapped in a corrupt environment that wants to eliminate him. Warlocks and wizards send these torrents of destruction against churches and ministries in order to knock them down and destroy them.

So shall they fear the name of the LORD from the west, and his glory from the rising of the sun. When the enemy shall come in like a flood, the Spirit of the LORD shall lift up a standard against him. Isaiah 59:19

Glory to God we have a Father in Heaven who is Almighty; not even the devil can forge weapons against us, and prevail over us:

Thus saith the LORD, thy redeemer, and he that formed thee from the womb, I am the LORD that maketh all things; that stretcheth forth the heavens alone; that spreadeth abroad the earth by myself; That frustrateth the tokens of the liars, and maketh diviners mad; that turneth wise men backward, and maketh their knowledge foolish; That confirmeth the word of his servant, and performeth the counsel of his messengers; that saith to Jerusalem, Thou shalt be inhabited; and to the cities of Judah, Ye shall be built, and I will raise up the decayed places thereof: That saith to the deep, Be dry, and I will dry up thy rivers: Isaiah 44:24-27

Maybe you find yourself in a similar situation regarding your health, finances, ministry or family. That is why I want you to notice a divine strategy in this passage. First of all, God awakens his words on King David's mouth. This means He wants to anoint him to undo the works of the devil that are drowning him. Therefore, the Lord undoes these torrents and rivers of perversity using our own voice to command these swamps to be dried from their very origin in the depths.

When you understand how iniquity works and how to uproot it from your life and your ways, the Glory of God will shine upon you and He will make covenant with your discordance.

And the Redeemer shall come to Zion, and unto them that turn from transgression in Jacob, saith the LORD. As for me, this is my covenant with them, saith the LORD; My spirit that is upon thee, and my words which I have put in thy mouth, shall not depart out of thy mouth, nor out of the mouth of thy seed, nor out of the mouth of thy seed's seed, saith the LORD, from henceforth and forever.   Isaiah 59:20-22

Iniquity produces Financial Ruin and Lack

As I said before, iniquity began in Lucifer's mind, when a twisted thought penetrated his heart, making him believe he could be similar to God. This happened due to the abundance of his riches. In Ezekiel chapters 27 and 28, the Bible describes the power of his commercial dealings and refers to him as the King of Tire, the capital of commerce at the time.

The fall of Lucifer is intimately tied to commerce and riches. It is from this love for riches that Babylon, the spiritual city where he governs the kingdoms of the world, emerges.

So he carried me away in the spirit into the wilderness: and I saw a woman sit upon a scarlet coloured beast, full of names of blasphemy, having seven heads and ten horns. And the woman was arrayed in purple and scarlet colour, and decked with gold and precious stones and pearls, having a golden cup in her hand full of abominations and filthiness of her fornication: And upon her forehead was a name written, MYSTERY, BABYLON THE GREAT, THE MOTHER OF HARLOTS AND ABOMINATIONS OF THE EARTH. And the woman which thou sawest is that great city, which reigneth over the kings of the earth.
Revelation 17:3-5 and 18

There is a part of trading and riches that is righteous and necessary for the people of the earth. Nevertheless, iniquity, the devil's seed, was used as fertile soil to sow his twisted evil nature.

All nations have participated in its seduction, and therefore, are trapped in its nets.

For all nations have drunk of the wine of the wrath of her fornication, and the kings of the earth have committed fornication with her, and the merchants of the earth are waxed rich through the abundance of her delicacies. And I heard another voice from heaven, saying, Come out of her, my people, that ye be not partakers of her sins, and that ye receive not of her plagues.   Revelation 18:3-4

Commerce and riches project such a splendor, that they have become the door for iniquity to enter. This splendor is a glory that it is not God's. It is a feeling of artificial security and power that rises up in order to take the place of God in the heart. It's brilliance charms and seduces the world.

The riches created in Lucifer's heart narcosis, a fascination for himself that made him believe the power of his wealth made him equal to the Most High.

By the multitude of thy merchandise they have filled the midst of thee with violence, and thou hast sinned: therefore I will cast thee as profane out of the mountain of God: and I will destroy thee, O covering cherub, from the midst of the stones of fire. Thine heart was lifted up because of thy beauty, thou hast corrupted thy wisdom by reason of thy brightness: I will cast thee to the ground, I

will lay thee before kings, that they may behold thee.
Ezekiel 28:16-17

Iniquity formed in the heart of Lucifer as a result of the beauty and splendor of his treasures, disturbed all his holy focus regarding riches. Everything was distorted in Him to the degree that His creator God became less important than the gold and precious stones. This distortion is the same satanic seed he is planting in the heart of men at their birth.

From the beginning of time, man, in his iniquity, has searched gold more than God. Commerce has been impregnated with iniquity in all possible forms. And, to some degree, this heritage is a constant issue in the bloodline of nearly all men.

Due to love for possessions, people have made war. Throughout the centuries, gold has been stained with blood. The one who owns the most wields power! This has been the slogan of every Western Civilization.

In almost every pagan culture, gold has been offered to the gods. Gold has always been the symbol of power in European kingdoms. All kinds of satanic covenants, witchcraft and high magic surround the riches of the world. The most abominable crime organizations have originated from love and quest for riches.

Even millions of Christians focus all their strengths searching for riches instead of pursuing God. When people are consumed with the goods and comforts of this world, the church reflects this iniquity forgetting the poor, homeless and widows. For some churches it is more important to worry about jewelry and dressings instead of caring about those who seem to be invisible.

For the church of God it has been a priority to obtain the riches of this world rather than offering its life to reach higher levels in God. We are full of iniquity! When our possessions, salary, or business have become our security, and not God, then we have fallen into the same trading that made Lucifer fall.

The economy of this world is full of iniquity and blood shedding. War is waged over money. Weapons are sold to terrorists, and entire nations are starving for the purpose of maintaining the market price. Bank systems are corrupt and full of lies and usury.

Governments sell their integrity for money. Justice is also corrupt. Gold is used to silence homicide and to pursue the forsaken. Fraud is conducted with citizens' money, in a system full of filth, fornication, robbery, lies and deceit. I do not believe I err if I say that most sins have money as a common denominator.

Whereas the devil weaves powerful blindfolds in order to justify all types of sin in the financial arena, God is being robbed at every turn in tithes and offerings. The one who lacks of money justifies himself in cheating and lying to his brother.

It is so easy for a person to borrow money from someone and not repay the debt, because money is more important than friendship.

It is on the subject of finances where I have found the least fear of God. And, what people are unaware of is that when we consume ourselves with money, and become its servants, we are signing a covenant with death. Notice how iniquity surrounding riches is intimately tied to spirits of death:

I will incline mine ear to a parable: I will open my dark saying upon the harp. Wherefore should I fear in the days of evil, when the iniquity of my heels shall compass me about? This their way is their folly: yet their posterity approve their sayings. Selah. Like sheep they are laid in the grave; death shall feed on them; and the upright shall have dominion over them in the morning; and their beauty shall consume in the grave from their dwelling. But God will redeem my soul from the power of the grave: for he shall receive me. Selah.

Psalm 49:4-5 and 13-15

Sheol is the place of the dead. However, in this psalm, we see how this place exercises an influence and power over those who are alive. Just like heaven exercises power over the just and the unjust, death is an empire that captivates those who are submitted to it through iniquity, rebellion, and sin.

Money should only be an instrument in our hands, However, it is for most people, a refuge that God has already begun to judge. This is why the Scriptures say, "Come out of her!" It is referring to the Babylonian system, which is this financial structure (Rev 18:4).

Because ye have said, we have made a covenant with death and with hell are we at agreement; when the overflowing scourge shall pass through, it shall not come unto us: for we have made lies our refuge, and under falsehood have we hid ourselves: Therefore, thus saith the Lord God. Behold I lay in Zion for a foundation a stone, a tried stone, a precious corner stone, a sure foundation: he hath believth shall not make haste. Judgment also will I lay to the line, and righteousness to the plummet: and the hail shall sweep away the refuge of lies, and the waters shall overflow the hiding place.   Isaiah 28:15-17

Trusting riches is not only attributed to the wealthy or powerful, but anyone who depends on money as a means of support or security. Financial iniquity attracts to itself judgments of ruin.

Therefore I will judge you, O house of Israel, every one according to his ways, saith the Lord GOD. Repent, and turn yourselves from all your transgressions; so iniquity shall not be your ruin. Ezekiel 18:30

I have seen this many times. Even in my own family I have seen how my grandfathers had a good financial position, but both ended up in ruin. When I became a Christian I had very little money and each time I received a financial blessing from the Lord, it was immediately snatched by the devil. In several occasions I was stripped of things that belonged to me legitimately. Even my parent's inheritance was taken from me righteously.

I didn't understand why I was losing my financial inheritance until I began to understand iniquity. Then, the course of my destiny changed. One day I asked the Lord to show me the financial iniquity in my lineage. Through a dream I saw one of my grandparents committing fraud with one of his business associates. This man cursed him and told him all his generations would be affected with financial ruins.

The next morning, when I woke up, the first thing I did was to ask forgiveness for the iniquity and sin of my grandfather and to cancel any curse, placing the sacrifice of Christ between my grandfather and his descendants. Then, I began to sound out the areas in which I had sinned by placing my confidence in riches or any other sin in the area of money that I could have committed. I asked for forgiveness. From day forward, God has returned to me everything the devil had stolen and the blessings of Jehovah rest upon my life.

As I said before, it was riches and commercial dealings which produced pride and eventually the fall of Lucifer. This is why he is always trying to infiltrate in this area of our lives. Therefore, it is important to analyze the origin and motive of each commercial transaction to detect any connection with iniquity that sooner or later will bring ruin to our life.

Examples of these are businesses that have been consecrated to idols, or people that have been stripped unrighteously. In other cases unclean money has been used or there was a partnership with someone who is a heathen, whose sin affected the business. Some businesses have been created with illegal merchandise, abuse towards employees, unfair measurements, false formulas or bribery to obtain permissions. Sometimes, one can sell fake products or can advertise one level of quality and deliver something less. Each case is diverse, but each one is worthy of examination.

Many people think God wants to bless them

financially regardless of the means. I have witnessed many ungodly transactions done to unbelievers by those calling themselves Christians, shielding themselves behind Proverbs 13:22, where it says the money of the sinners will pass to the hands of the righteous.

Nowadays, many marketing methods are filled with lies and deceit, in order to trap the client. God takes all of this very seriously and it prevents Him from hearing our prayers.

Behold, the LORD's hand is not shortened, that it cannot save; neither his ear heavy, that it cannot hear: But your iniquities have separated between you and your God, and your sins have hid his face from you, that he will not hear. For your hands are defiled with blood, and your fingers with iniquity; your lips have spoken lies, your tongue hath muttered perverseness. None calleth for justice, nor any pleadeth for truth: they trust in vanity, and speak lies; they conceive mischief, and bring forth iniquity.   *Isaiah 59:1-5*

When inquiring about iniquity, I found some things that appear to be noble. However, the origin is unjust. As we said before, buying, selling or having a business is not wrong, but an excessive profit that causes inflation becomes iniquity. When this happens, the person is being seduced by greed, making a necessary product difficult to obtain by people.

There are some Christians who promote multilevel companies and stop seeing the church as God's family. Instead it is a source for their profits. These people no longer relate to other people for love of service to God, but because they represent a satisfactory income. This is iniquity. The problem here is not the multilevel, but the companies self serving purpose for them to have communion with the holy ones.

God wants to give us abundant blessings and he will, as soon as we become the answer to help our neighbors' solve their problems.

In order to be free from iniquity, we must confess our sins and iniquity, and in the cases where we have offended someone, it is necessary to have restoration, if at all possible. In case we are involved in wrongdoing, we must cease immediately. If we do not, sooner or later, ruin will visit us and our descendants.

Iniquity and stubbornness

For rebellion is as the sin of witchcraft, and stubbornness is as iniquity and idolatry. Because thou hast rejected the word of the LORD, he hath also rejected thee from being king. And Saul said unto Samuel, I have sinned: for

I have transgressed the commandment of the LORD, and thy words: because I feared the people, and obeyed their voice.   *1 Samuel 15:23-24*

Pride, which goes hand in hand with tenacity, was the sin that introduced iniquity in Lucifer's heart. Someone who is obstinate or stubborn will make his own opinion an idol. This way of thinking gets so strong when founded in a certain tradition or theological way of thinking that people no longer allow God to take part. This is the case of the Pharisee and the religious man of this era; they have made themselves idols of their own doctrines and have become blind and deaf to God's voice.

The Lord is continuously revealing new things and giving us light over others that we only knew partially. God can transform or complete methods and revelations that were glorious in the past, which perhaps are the core of any revival.

If we are so tied to a certain way of thinking or even to a revelation or doctrine, that we do not allow God to touch, then we are facing obstinacy as an iniquity and we need to repent. God is to reign completely in our lives.

We must keep a humble heart before God and allow Him to mold us and use us as he wishes.

Iniquity and the devastation of cities

Iniquity not only affects a person's life, but it constitutes the foundation for the curse and the destruction of cities. Since men originally sinned, iniquity entered mankind and took part of all his being. The earth absorbed this evil seed and was cursed from that moment on.

And unto Adam he said, because thou hast hearkened unto the voice of thy wife, and hast eaten of the tree, of which I commanded thee, saying, Thou shalt not eat of it: cursed is the ground for thy sake; in sorrow shalt thou eat of it all the days of thy life.   *Genesis 3:17*

From that moment on, the whole creation groans too see the manifestation of the sons of God. The Lord gave us the earth and, even though man lost the lordship over it, today it is our responsibility to declare its redemption through the sacrifice Jesus did for us. Although the human being was responsible for the curse on the land, today we can be a blessing for it and eat from its fruits with peace and joy.

Iniquity not only penetrated the earth in the moment of the fall of man, but also our individual iniquity brings all kinds of evil upon it.

Do ye indeed speak righteousness, O congregation? do ye

judge uprightly, O ye sons of men? Yea, in heart ye work wickedness; ye weigh the violence of your hands in the earth.   Psalms 58:1-2

Entire cities are founded through the territorial consecration of pagan gods, masonic designs, geometric magic, and horrible bloodshed sacrifices. All of these things reverberate in the development of a city, being necessary to redeem its foundations to transform it.

Woe to him that buildeth a town with blood, and stablisheth a city by iniquity!   Habakkuk 2:12

Just as iniquity digs holes to trap the souls of people; complete cities are submitted and sunken in darkness, violence and corruption.

The heathen are sunk down in the pit that they made: in the net which they hid is their own foot taken.
                                                          Psalms 9:15

This is why it is necessary for just people to make justice on the earth, so that their operation and deeds will heal the land.

If they shall confess their iniquity, and the iniquity of their fathers, with their trespass which they trespassed against me, and that also they have walked contrary unto me; And that I also have walked contrary unto them, and have brought them into the land of their enemies; if then their uncircumcised hearts be humbled, and they then accept of the punishment of their iniquity: Then will I remember my covenant with Jacob, and also my covenant with Isaac, and also my covenant with Abraham will I remember; and I will remember the land.

Leviticus 26:40-42

Cultural Iniquity

Iniquity also comes from our culture. Men's collective actions of evil, for instance, the genocide that the Spaniards and Portuguese committed towards the Latin–American Indians or the terrible massacres done by the British when they conquered the United States, were indirectly rooted in the soul and the spirit of the nations.

We can also mention the Spanish Inquisition or the uncountable deaths produced by the crusades in Europe and the Middle East. All these acts of bloodshed are iniquity that remained stamped in our spiritual inheritance.

On the other hand, we have the iniquity that is inherent to the idiosyncrasy (thought) of a nation. The corruption and indolence in Latin America, along with the irresponsibility and fraudulent ways to those things, are clear examples of these. They are so rooted and common for us, that we do not even notice that they are iniquity.

Thoughts such as: "the end justifies the means." "They are not going to realize it" and so many other sayings, reflect how our society is bound to iniquity. Lies, deception, and shame are part of the iniquity in many nations.

People make agreements with the devil every time we call something wrong as good or something good as wrong. Another example of this is when we accept abominable rituals and traditions that belong to our culture, and we even buy figures of ancestral civilizations full of demons.

Celebrations such as "Halloween", "the Day of the Deaths", "the Roman Saturnalias" disguised in Christmas, the Easter party which is infected of syncretism with the little rabbits and chocolate eggs, are all rituals.

If we make a list of those aspects in which we are tied to iniquity as nations with their own culture, this would be endless. Each person has to ask God forgiveness for the sins of their own nation, and purge out of their life all acts and iniquities that are in their blood due to their culture and race.

Religious Iniquity

Religions are loaded with iniquity for they are deeds of death. Any religious system is, by essence, Babylonian and is opposed to the one true God. Those who come from a religious background have to uproot from their hearts the iniquity that entered through religious ceremonies and traditions.

Those who come from the Roman system must break all bounds with idolatry, magic and occultism. It is not enough to just stop our old habits. We must cleanse ourselves from the iniquity that has been soaked in our spirit.

And there came one of the seven angels which had the seven vials, and talked with me, saying unto me, Come hither; I will shew unto thee the judgment of the great whore that sitteth upon many waters: With whom the kings of the earth have committed fornication, and the inhabitants of the earth have been made drunk with the wine of her fornication.   *Revelations 17:1-2*

We must break the pacts done with these demons. *What say I then? that the idol is any thing, or that which is offered in sacrifice to idols is any thing? But I say, that the things which the Gentiles sacrifice, they sacrifice to devils, and not to God: and I would not that ye should have fellowship with devils. Ye cannot drink the cup of the Lord, and the cup of devils: ye cannot be partakers of the Lord's table, and of the table of devils. Do we provoke the Lord to jealousy? are we stronger than he?*

1 Corinthians 10:19-22

Not only are the pagan religions plagued with iniquity but also current Christianity. When I wrote my book related to the Masonry: "The Dark Secret of GAOTU"[2], I realized that many pastors, bishops, and members of the Traditional Evangelic Church are involved in this order (Baptists, Methodists, Presbyterian, Episcopalians).

Most of them are being taught lies and ignore what really happens in the higher realms of this Order. However, they are not exempt from all of its curses and torrents of perversity that they are bringing to their lives.

Freemasonry is a disguised cult to Lucifer. When a Pastor is deceived and participates with this fraternity all his sheep enter under a masonic leadership. (I recommend reading my book on Freemasonry in order to be released from all these pacts and curses). I want to make clear that not all the pastors within traditional churches are part of this secret society.

On the other hand, there are people who have belonged to Eastern religions following their gods and traditions. If this is the case and all those pacts most be broken in order to be set free.

Iniquity and affront

An affront is an injustice done to someone and, as a consequence, the person remains in grief and dishonor. It is an insult or attack of injustice that affects the very core of the person. It is marked by an offense that destroys essential parts of the "heart." It is an impartation of iniquity into the most inner being.

The presence of an affront in a person's life acts as a powerful magnet, attracting offenses and injustices. One way this kind of iniquity manifests itself is through the tongue. Our tongue determines many of the curses or blessings we receive.

Death and life are in the power of the tongue: and they that love it shall eat the fruit thereof.
Proverbs 18:21

The tongue expresses what is in the heart, as illustrated by the apostle Luke:
...for of the abundance of the heart his mouth speaketh.
Luke 6:45b

A heart weighed down with iniquity continually talks negatively about other people. These people are not careful in how they express themselves, either through profanity or cursing. They create division and offend others, as if they had daggers in their mouths. These people are negative, exclusivists, and have a heart full of rage and bitterness.

This is the result of multiple offenses and injustices that continually plague them. This type of iniquity produces a vicious cycle of destroying and being destroyed.

People, who have been rejected, appear to attract more and more rejection. This happens because they are trapped in nets of iniquity. There is a spiritual law in operation, and this law will continue until iniquity is removed from their lineage.

These people have been abused in some way, either incestuously or psychological, and become victims of injustice. They attract affront and dishonor to their life, as if they wear a bull's-eye on their back.

In the case of incest (sexual relations with a family member), iniquity is so strong that it attracts all kinds of curses, such as those described in Deuteronomy 28. The abused person must forgive and ask for forgiveness for the sins of his ancestors. Certainly, there are many similar cases in the family lineages, which brought this influence on the father or a family member to commit this aberration.

Have the workers of iniquity no knowledge? who eat up my people as they eat bread: they have not called upon God.   *Psalm 53:4*

In order to stop this cycle of injustice and affront, one must inquire in his or her heart, identifying those occasions when we have been unjust towards other people. Then, if you do not know the instance where this sin and iniquity originated ask for revelation. Also, ask God for forgiveness for the iniquity of your ancestors. When our tongue has slandered and abused someone, causing pain and inflicting deep wounds restitution is necessary. Repentance before God is the first step, but this will not remove the seed of iniquity that you have sown against yourself You must bring restitution for what you have done in the past. You must do something good for them in order to undo the evil that you have caused.

Wash you, make you clean; put away the evil of your doings from before mine eyes; cease to do evil; Learn to do well; seek judgment, relieve the oppressed, judge the fatherless, plead for the widow.

Isaiah 1:16-17

Iniquity and the Spirit of Fornication

Bowing and serving strange gods is a work of iniquity that God hates. In Latin America, gods are made of sculptures and pictures. In Europe and in North America these gods are money, comfort and culture, although images are also worshipped.

Unfortunately, idolatry is the beginning of a series of sins directed by the spirit of fornication. Nowadays, nations are overrun with bold licentiousness and sexual depravation as never before. Even in the Church sins of adultery, pornography and fornication are proliferating for there is no fear of God anymore.

I feel my heart flagging for this cause, because I see churches with great knowledge in the Word, anointing, prophecy and other gifts of God. Yet, Christians seem to be so hardened, nothing makes them change.

Of course, there are beautiful people in Christ, holy and fearful of God. But the majority remains fearless, because the nations are full of idolatrous iniquity. At least in Latin America people who have left wooden idols, remain trapped by this spirit of fornication that prevents them from knowing God fully.

Whoredom and wine and new wine take away the heart. My people ask counsel at their stocks, and their staff declareth unto them: for the spirit of whoredoms hath caused them to err, and they have gone a whoring from under their God. They sacrifice upon the tops of the mountains, and burn incense upon the hills, under oaks and poplars and elms, because the shadow thereof is good: therefore your daughters shall commit whoredom, and your spouses shall commit adultery. I will not punish your daughters when they commit whoredom, nor your spouses when they commit adultery: for themselves are separated with whores, and they sacrifice with harlots: therefore the people that doth not understand shall fall... They will not frame their doings to turn unto their God: for the spirit of whoredoms is in the midst of them, and they have not known the LORD.

Hosea 4:11-14 and 5:4

Note that where there is or has been idolatry, the spirit of fornication is loosed. That's why it is important to uproot iniquity in depth and precision. General repentance is superficial, but if the root and the essence of the problem are left untreated, sooner or later, sexual sins will manifest.

Fornication is not only physical, but also a condition of the heart infected with iniquity that prevents people from knowing God intimately and embracing Him wholeheartedly. We can see people who want pleasant experiences with the Holy Spirit. They desire the warmth of a relationship, but not the commitment of a marriage with God.

This type of iniquity causes people to be pursued continually by sexual dreams and vile and obscene thoughts. I have known people desperate to escape this situation, who have no idea what to do in order to be free.

The solution is to take a pen and a paper, and write a detailed list of idols adored by themselves or family members. Take notes on the pacts made with such images or spirits, and also promises or gifts made. Ask God to forgive you and your ancestors for this iniquity and command it to be uprooted from your life.

In addition, you must identify all situations in which you had sexual interaction outside marriage, for example, fornication, pornography, masturbation, incest, adultery, etc. It is important to be specific. If a person has had a promiscuous life, it may be difficult to remember all of the names. However, all of this information is registered in our spirit and the Holy Spirit is able to remind us of each instance.

Perhaps he will do it all at once, or it may take weeks. That's fine. The important thing is to do it.

Then, we will enjoy a beautiful liberty and powerful intimacy with our beloved Lord. Once this is completed, it is important to declare the freedom for our descendants.

Iniquity and Curses

Blessings as well as curses, are spiritual laws searching for places to land. They are like a bird in flight looking for a place to nest in order to establish and fulfill its purpose.

As the bird by wandering, as the swallow by flying, so the curse causeless shall not come.   Proverbs 26:2

At the same time, we see in Deuteronomy chapter 28:2, 15

And all these blessings shall come on thee, and overtake thee, if thou shalt hearken unto the voice of the LORD thy God. But it shall come to pass, if thou wilt not hearken unto the voice of the LORD thy God, to observe to do all his commandments and his statutes which I command thee this day; that all these curses shall come upon thee, and overtake thee.

Many times I find people who, after having read books or hearing teachings about curses, revoke them and cancel them in their lives, but over time they return. The reason is the power of the Spirit succeeded in removing them for a time, but their cause, which was actually iniquity, was never uprooted.

As we said before, if we imagine the form of iniquity, it would look like a twisted, black cord inside of us, made of hundreds of knots, and layered upon layer, making it thick. These layers are like filthy rags, full of information and covenants that have been accumulated from generation to generation. Large quantities of curses cling to this cord, as well as decrees we make along with our ancestors.

The sin of Judah is written with a pen of iron, and with the point of a diamond: it is graven upon the table of their heart, and upon the horns of your altars...
Jeremiah 17:1

This body of iniquity records all of the sins committed by prior generations, and it is precisely from this information that sin grows and manifests itself. This information is not removed through a general prayer, such as, "Lord erase all my iniquities." Sin, rebellion and iniquity require observation and an exhaustive analysis of our heart.

Although in the sincere prayer of a genuine conversion many sins where not confessed, Jesus takes our repentant heart to give us salvation. However, from that point on, the Holy Spirit begins to reform our conscience; illuminating our understanding about sins that we have not even acknowledged as such. He will cause us to repent of sins in our lives that we were never ashamed of before because we were ignorant about them. As far as we are docile and lay out our hearts to the Lord, He will lead us to repentance in each area needed for our sanctification.

He deals with our iniquities in the same way, since it is here that the root of our problem is found and more demonic activity is woven.

Blessed is the man unto whom the LORD imputeth not iniquity, and in whose spirit there is no guile. When I kept silence, my bones waxed old through my roaring all the day long. For day and night thy hand was heavy upon me: my moisture is turned into the drought of summer. Selah. I acknowledge my sin unto thee, and mine iniquity have I not hid. I said, I will confess my transgressions unto the LORD; and thou forgavest the iniquity of my sin. Selah.   *Psalm 32:2-5*

Note how the redemptive work of God goes to the very depths of the matter, to the very place where sin originated. If we deal with sin only in a superficial manner, the body of iniquity will continue to thrive.

When studying iniquity in relation to curses, it is necessary to identify through prayer the root of iniquity that produced such curses, and then uproot them one at a time.

What is a curse?

I like the definition given by the Apostle John Eckhardt in his book "Identifying And Breaking Curses"[3]: "A curse is the penalty given by God to a person and to his descendants as the result of their iniquity."

Render unto them a recompence, O LORD, according to the work of their hands. Give them sorrow of heart, thy curse unto them.   Lamentations 3:64-65

Curses can be defined through several recurring symptoms that spring from specific roots of iniquity: **chronic financial problems, poverty and misery, land that does not produce fruit, businesses that dry up with no apparent reason.**

Cause: Robbery, fraud, witchcraft, idolatry, trusting in man before God, robbing God of tithes and offerings (Malachi 3:8–9), swearing falsely in the name of God (Zechariah 5:4).

Gynecologic problems in the woman: continual flow of blood, chronic menstrual disorders, sterility and miscarriage.

Cause: Incest, adultery, divorce, sexual perversion, abortion, pornography, fornication, sexual abuse, rebellion and disobedience (Genesis 3:16).

Chronic or diverse illnesses, one after another.

Cause: Idolatry, witchcraft, blood shedding (Deuteronomy 28:27 and 35).

Fungus problems on the skin or nails, fevers and causalities.

Cause: Witchcraft, filthy practices, curses cast upon a person (Deuteronomy 28:22).

Accident Prone.

Cause: Homicide, death, blood shedding, worship of death, spiritualism, witchcraft, idolatry and satanism (Deuteronomy 28).

Marital problems, divorce and a disloyal spouse.

Cause: Divorce, disloyalty, idolatry, witchcraft, incest and adultery (Deuteronomy 28:30).

Premature death and suicide.

Cause: Homicide, blood shedding, idolatry, witchcraft and the love of money (Proverbs 2:22, Psalm 37:28).

Problems of continual robbery, fraud, frozen inheritances, loss of houses or properties.

Cause: Robbery, fraud, illegal traffic of merchandise, slave's trade or white slavery (Zechariah 5:3-4).

Mental problems, insanity, Alzheimer's and senile dementia.

Cause: Pride, haughtiness, trusting in riches and stubbornness (Daniel 4:32, Deuteronomy 28:18).

Destruction of different natures.

Cause: Homicide, violence, drunkenness, drug addiction, witchcraft, idolatry and suicide (Deuteronomy 28:20).

Affront and abuse of all kinds.

Cause: Rape, abuse, slander and a slanderous tongue (Psalm 53:4).

Becoming a wanderer or a vagabond, being thrown out of one's own country, living as an illegal in a foreign land.

Cause: Homicide and trusting in riches (Genesis 4:12 and Psalm 109:10).

Defeat before one's enemies.

Cause: Idolatry, witchcraft and rebellion (Deuteronomy 28:25).

When someone detects that he is under a curse, the first thing he must do is determine the cause. This can be found in himself or his lineage. Usually it is found in both. Sometimes we need the Holy Spirit to reveal to us things from the past, as in the case I related about my grandfather in the segment "iniquity and the ruin".

Next, you must repent of that specific iniquity, and uproot it from your spirit by means of a declaration. Once this is done, you must revoke and cancel the curses, breaking their power over your life. To conclude, proclaim upon your life the victory where He was made a curse to set us free.

Christ hath redeemed us from the curse of the law, being made a curse for us: for it is written, Cursed is every one that hangeth on a tree: That the blessing of Abraham might come on the Gentiles through Jesus Christ; that we might receive the promise of the Spirit through faith.

Galatians 3:13-14

5

The Power of Attraction of Spiritual Powers

Righteousness and iniquity are spiritual forces that have a tremendous force of attraction on themselves. The first one is intrinsically tied to the throne of God, and the other, to the devil's. Righteousness is an attribute of the Lord that aligns everything up with the Kingdom of God. On the other hand, iniquity is the force that twists and perverts everything, separating it from the designs of God.

Jesus, desiring to teach us a powerful truth, tells us in his Word:

Therefore I say unto you, Take no thought for your life, what ye shall eat, or what ye shall drink; nor yet for your body, what ye shall put on. Is not the life more

than meat, and the body than raiment? Therefore take
no thought, saying, What shall we eat? or, What shall we
drink? or, Wherewithal shall we be clothed? (For after
all these things do the Gentiles seek:) for your heavenly
Father knoweth that ye have need of all these things. But
seek ye first the kingdom of God, and his righteousness;
and all these things shall be added unto you.

Matthew 6:25 and 31-33

Here we can see that if we approach the kingdom
of God and His righteousness, a power of attraction
is produced drawing all things of His kingdom towards
us. The righteousness of God contains within itself a
powerful force that continually judges iniquity,
fighting against it in order to align everything with
God.

On the other hand, this force also pulls everything
that has to do with the Kingdom of heaven, and all
blessings from above. It pulls towards itself all
spiritual and material riches. This is because
righteousness is intimately tied to the glory of God;
because they go hand in hand, manifesting themselves
simultaneously.

The heavens declare his righteousness, and all the
people see his glory.   *Psalm 97:6*

Isaiah talks about this magnetic power and it's

manifestation in the believer who is established in the righteousness of God and has become a vessel of God's glory.

Arise, shine; for your light has come, And the glory of the LORD has risen upon you. For behold, darkness will cover the earth And deep darkness the peoples; But the LORD will rise upon you And His glory will appear upon you. Nations will come to your light, And kings to the brightness of your rising. Lift up your eyes round about and see; They all gather together, they come to you Your. Your sons will come from afar, And your daughters will be carried in the arms. Then you will see and be radiant, And your heart will thrill and rejoice; Because the abundance of the sea will be turned to you, The wealth of the nations will come to you. Isaiah 60:1-5 (NASB)

Notice how the blessings are drawn to the very place where the glory of God is seen. This glory can only manifest itself when righteousness has begun its transforming power in a child of God. This goes much further than being just, it is by grace. This righteousness, which is by faith, is our passport into heaven.

In order for the glory to exercise its power of attraction over all the blessings and attributes of the kingdom of heaven on this earth, it is necessary for the righteousness of God to remove iniquity from our being. The glory of God immerses us in everything God is; it is not a beautiful glitter that makes us feel good. Different from the anointing, that is the ability to fill us with joy and love, the glory is the consuming fire of God. The Glory burns and destroys everything that separates us from God.

Many want the dimensions of His Glory without ever having identified and uprooted the terrible weight of iniquity within them. Prolonged suffering can be the result of approaching His glory in this manner, for they do not know what is happening.

Now then, entering into His fire is a necessary step in the ways of God, since without His glory and righteousness, we would never possess our inheritance of blessing, power and all kinds of additions found in His kingdom.

In order to achieve our sanctification, iniquity must be identified and eliminated. This is a fundamental part of the victory in the cross. Then, two virtues of the Almighty operate: righteousness and glory, which are fundamental aspects of His Kingdom that polish us and also bring judgment upon our enemies.

The LORD reigns, let the earth rejoice; Let the many islands be glad. Clouds and thick darkness surround Him; Righteousness and justice are the foundation of His throne. Fire goes before Him And burns up His adversaries round about.   *Psalm 97:1-3*

It is important to understand that just as the love of God cannot stop loving, the righteousness of God cannot stop judging. In divine terms, God's judgments are sent in order to establish His righteousness. The Lord's judgments are aligning things with His perfect will and essence. In this process He uses correcting judgments, revealing judgments and, in extreme cases, destructive judgments.

What does righteousness judge?

It precisely judges iniquity. This is where everything that has been perverted from the ways of God is established. Wherever iniquity is found, we will continuously find God's judgments manifested.

Now, just as righteousness and God's glory exercise a magnetic power over everything pertaining to the kingdom of God, iniquity exercises that same power, but with the opposite results. As if a giant magnet, iniquity will draw everything that has to do with the empire of death and darkness to itself.

Iniquity is the legal bases used by the devil to release evil upon the human being and, even more, the believer. Now you can see how important this topic is, as it is the bull's-eye for the devil's bombs and the bull's-eye for the judgments of God.

God establishes His Righteousness with Mercy for those who seek Him.

The topic of God's judgments scares most people. However, it is wrong to think that every time God acts in this manner something terrible is going to happen.

In my book "Seated in Heavenly Places"[4] I discuss this matter. But, in order to give birth to the ones who have not read it, I dare to talk about it in this occasion.

The first thing we must understand is God loves us deeply and He is always thinking about what is best for His children. For this reason, He desires His glory and righteousness to be established in our lives, so that all of His blessings will come upon us, and we will live in abundance, peace and joy, delighting in our beloved heavenly Father.

God acts through judgments of mercy upon those who fear Him and seek His righteousness.

I love them that love me; and those that seek me early shall find me. Riches and honour are with me; yea, durable riches and righteousness. My fruit is better than gold, yea, than fine gold; and my revenue than choice silver. I lead in the way of righteousness, in the midst of the paths of judgment: That I may cause those that love me to inherit substance; and I will fill their treasures.

Proverbs 8:17-21

It is such a blessing when God with His judgments straightens out all that is twisted, wrong or badly structured. In order to accomplish this purpose, God uses judgments of mercy. These judgments are all of the circumstances and words that He speaks into our life, dreams and moments of divine lucidity that allow us to see our wrong ways and turn to his ways.

The powerful work of God in our lives will establish us as "righteous" on the earth with all the privileges this affords. There is a difference between being declared "righteous" by grace through the sacrifice of Jesus, and being established in righteousness.

All the blessings, honor, and riches, do not come flooding from heaven toward us after our baptism, but in the measure that we are rooted and grounded in righteousness.

King David clearly understood this principle, and he knew that his victories depended upon the righteousness of God being established in him.

Arise, O LORD, in thine anger, lift up thyself because of the rage of mine enemies: and awake for me to the judgment that thou hast commanded. The LORD shall judge the people: judge me, O LORD, according to my righteousness, and according to mine integrity that is in me. Oh let the wickedness of the wicked come to an end; but establish the just...   *Psalm 7:6 and 8-9 a*

He also understood that the judgments of God were sweet and wonderful because they brought him closer to his beloved Lord. When you love God with all your heart and strength, anything that hinders your communion with Him is unbearable, and you want it removed as soon as possible.

There are things that we are aware of and others that are so hidden inside of us that revelation becomes necessary.

The statutes of the LORD are right, rejoicing the heart: the commandment of the LORD is pure, enlightening the eyes. The fear of the LORD is clean, enduring for ever: the judgments of the LORD are true and righteous altogether. More to be desired are they than gold, yea, than much fine gold: sweeter also than honey and the honeycomb.   *Psalm 19:8-10*

God shows the prophet Malachi how Jesus longs to refine us with all of His love. The Lord wants to do a perfect work in all of us in order to accomplish His perfect work. He must cleanse and polish us.

But who may abide the day of his coming? and who shall stand when he appeareth? for he is like a refiner's fire, and like fullers' soap: And he shall sit as a refiner and purifier of silver: and he shall purify the sons of Levi, and purge them as gold and silver, that they may offer unto the LORD an offering in righteousness.   Malachi 3:2-3

The tribe of Levi represents the priesthood of His house, the holy priests. We all have been constituted by Jesus. The mere fact that He seeks to refine us speaks to me of a work done with care, dedication and love. God purifies us in this way, but not everyone has the love and meekness required for this cleansing process to be accomplished.

God wants to discipline others as a father corrects his children. Unfortunately, He will have to punish many others to make their way straight and save them from death. It is impossible to have the blessings of God and to participate in His glory without being first confronted with our iniquities.

6

The Righteousness Free us from Iniquity

The fundamental principles of the faith exposed in this chapter are treated in a different form from what it is taught nowadays. They are developed under a prophetic and apostolic understanding that founds us like a building in God, able to contain His last glory.

1. – Justification from the focus of a new Apostolic Reformation

It would be impossible talking about iniquity and how to be free from it, without understanding clearly the justifying sacrifice of Christ in the Calvary. Many false interpretations have been made when trying to understand this foundation that keeps thousands of people blind, believing they have a salvation they actually have not acquired.

God is restoring all things and one of the most important things is the preaching of the true Word of God, in all its power and majesty.

I deeply believe in the redemptive work of God in my life, that is why I live. I believe in his absolute, redemptive, and healing power. I believe that we are saved by grace through the faith in Him; a faith that gives fruit and powerful deeds in God. But I also believe we have diluted the preaching of the gospel so much, in order to bring people to God's feet, that we have lost the basic ingredients of Salvation.

We have reduced His transforming and confronting gospel, into a sweet and simple "prayer of the sinner" that lacks of spiritual life and commitment with the Lord. A prayer in which a great amount of people that pray it do not have the minimal conviction of sin neither a desire to start living for Jesus and depart from the world.

We make them lots of promises, making them believe all of God's blessings will come upon them because they are now righteous people, although their lives are full of injustice. The truth is that most of these churches live endless defeats; they walk in deserts never ending, "having the name they live, but being death."

Justification through faith originates when I believe with all my heart that Jesus has taken my sins to the cross and I put my life on that cross to live for him: when I make the decision to leave my old way of living behind because I'm truly repentant and ashamed of all the deeds that made Jesus go through a terrible and painful sacrifice.

The union with Christ is like a marriage. In fact, Paul makes this comparison in his epistle to the Galatians. When someone marries, he leaves his old way of living as single, leaves his parents' house and unites to his woman. The same happens when we become one with Christ. We stop living as we did in the past and unite in the same Spirit with the Lord.

However, in most cases, people live a gospel with compromise, where living in the old sinful structure is irrelevant. It is such a common belief that they have been justified by grace and that they will enter into the Kingdom of God despite what they do, because they spoke with their mouth: "Lord, come to live in my heart". This is a dangerous lie.

Although grace is an undeserved gift from God,

and salvation requires no effort from us, IT IS a requirement to enter the kingdom of God through the CROSS. We have no other choice; this is the NARROW DOOR that leads us to salvation. It is on the cross where the repentent soul gives his life with the firm purpose to start a new life, leaving behind the old habits of sin or the futile and sinful way of living in the past.

Enter ye in at the strait gate: for wide is the gate, and broad is the way, that leadeth to destruction, and many there be which go in thereat: Because strait is the gate, and narrow is the way, which leadeth unto life, and few there be that find it. Matthew 7:13-14

2. – What is to invoke the name of the Lord?

To invoke the name of the Lord is powerful, but involves an action from us. To invoke means "to call inside" This is calling the Spirit of the Living God to come to us and unite with our spirit.

This step, essential for our salvation, may be done in God's way, for it is the foundation of our faith:

Nevertheless the foundation of God standeth sure, having this seal; The Lord knoweth them that are his. And, let everyone that nameth the name of Christ depart from iniquity. 2 Timothy 2:19

I consider this aspect essential. So, I ask you to open your heart in order to understand in a deep way a truth that has been treated lightly by most churches nowadays.

The first fact that we must understand, is how important it is for us to depart from iniquity in order to receive the Holy Spirit in us. Once He has come upon us, we must stand firm in Him so as to remain in holiness.

Everyone wants to be sealed by the Holy Spirit of the promise, but this seal is established when invoking the name of Christ with a true heart. It does not happen with a simple prayer done in ignorance. It requires a step of complete conviction in which we decide with all of our heart to turn from our own ways and iniquity, towards God's justice.

For with the heart man believeth unto righteousness; and with the mouth confession is made unto salvation.
Romans 10:10

3.- We are to believe with the heart, not with the mind.

Believing with the heart involves the firm determination to walk in the justice that comes from God, and take from His grace all the power we need to completely become His justice. It is not just saying "I believe in God", and doing whatever I want because God considers me righteous anyway. James refers to this way of belief as useless, for it does not go along with the deeds of the faith. He says:

Thou believest that there is one God; thou doest well: the devils also believe, and tremble. But wilt thou know, O vain man, that faith without works is dead?

James 2:19-20

It is in the heart where the system of beliefs is found. The heart is the only one that has the inner strength to determine a change of direction in our ways. The mind reflects and accepts, but lacks the power to break structures of behavior. Determined decisions in our life can only be taken in the heart; otherwise, they will just be an emotion of the moment.

Watchman Nee[5], the famous theologian from the last century, wrote in his book "The Spiritual Man": Everything that belongs to the natural man, for instance, the "I" of the believer, must die in the cross. If the meaning of this is considered just as an idea or a concept, maybe my reason will accept it, but as it is something we must practice, the mind will reject it immediately.

Only the heart may establish the decision to enter

God by the cross, humiliate, obey, and leave the pleasures and rudiments of this world. Dr. Nee also states in his book: "Many people consider themselves Christians, but what they actually believe is philosophy, ethic and doctrines about the truth or some supernatural phenomena. Believing in such a way does not produce a new birth nor gives people a new spirit."[6]

When we just believe with our mind, we can know the Bible or recite the creed by heart, but none of these things entail a new birth. It is through the heart. The heart is the only organ intimately bound to our spirit through which we can truly repent and have a radical change in our life.

4.– It is necessary to leave our sinful way of living

The Apostle John also talks about this emphasizing that walking in iniquity and believing oneself righteous is a deception. Let us remember that iniquity and justice are completely opposed to each other. If they both were to inhabit together a believer's life, he will find himself in a deplorable state of judgment his whole life, because justice is continuously judging iniquity:

And ye know that he was manifested to take away our

sins; and in him is no sin. Whosoever abideth in him sinneth not: whosoever sinneth hath not seen him, neither known him. Little children, let no man deceive you: he that doeth righteousness IS RIGHTEOUS, even as he is righteous. He that committeth sin is of the devil; for the devil sinneth from the beginning. For this purpose the Son of God was manifested, that he might destroy the works of the devil. Whosoever is born of God doth not commit sin; for his seed remaineth in him: and he cannot sin, because he is born of God. In this the children of God are manifest, and the children of the devil: whosoever doeth not righteousness is not of God, neither he that loveth not his brother.   *1 John 3: 5-10*

When the son of God manifests in the heart of a man who has sincerely invoked his name, something powerful happens. Christ will arise with power in order to undo all the iniquity and deeds the devil has built in the true believer.

John, who deeply understands the action of the divine seed engendered in man, knows without doubt that Christ's presence in the spirit and in the heart of a someone, will keep him away from sin. Therefore, the devil shall not be able to touch God's people.

We know that whosoever is born of God sinneth not; but he that is begotten of God keepeth himself, and that wicked one toucheth him not.   *1 John 5:18*

The gospel is a call to a genuine conversion, which literally takes us from the kingdom of darkness into the Light. When the apostle Paul converts on his way to Damascus, the Lord talks to him very clearly about his call, telling him:

But rise, and stand upon thy feet: for I have appeared unto thee for this purpose, to make thee a minister and a witness both of these things which thou hast seen, and of those things in the which I will appear unto thee; Delivering thee from the people, and from the Gentiles, unto whom now I send thee, To open their eyes, and to turn them from darkness to light, and from the power of Satan unto God, that they may receive forgiveness of sins, and inheritance among them which are sanctified by faith that is in me.   *Acts 26:16-18*

The fact that the Lord uses the Word "to transfer" entails a change of locality, that is to say, we cannot be in two places at the same time. To transfer means leaving a place in order to move to another. People who want to be in Christ and the world at the same time, have actually never been transferred, they have never left Satan's legal authority.

It is necessary that their eyes be opened for them to see the condition of their soul in relation to God, so that they may decide to leave the darkness.

After this process they will be able to BE TRANSFERRED to the light.

5. – Are all those who claim to be saved truly saved?

The true gospel is the authentic power of God taking us from a vain, carnal and innocuous way of living, and producing new powerful creatures full of His glory.

When God started to pour His apostolic anointing upon my life, I started to see the Word as never before . The Lord started an authentic reformation inside of me. This revelation has drawn me to reread the Bible several times , restructuring fundamental truths that in the past , I had accepted just in a pragmatic way as I had been taught.

I never wondered about the way I was taught, until the evidence of a church, in a vast majority, sinking in sin and the pain that I felt for it, lead me to go deeper in the Scriptures.

For as I live a holy life I know that God's seed and the life in the Spirit, do not relate with a life in iniquity and sin. Nowadays, the church wants to make people who have never truly repented, heirs of God's promises. These people want what is best from both worlds. They want all the blessings from God but also the pleasures of this world. Today, the church calls "sons of God, born again" to fornicators, adulterers, cheaters, robbers, people full of pride, pornography, abuse, and frauds. Nowadays, we call people baptized in the Holy Spirit, who abound in lust, deception, witchery, and idolatry. They are people who do not even feel guilty when they slander or defame the precious Body of Christ.

Know ye not that the unrighteous shall not inherit the kingdom of God? Be not deceived: neither fornicators, nor idolaters, nor adulterers, nor effeminate, nor abusers of themselves with mankind, Nor thieves, nor covetous, nor drunkards, nor revilers, nor extortioners, shall inherit the kingdom of God.   *1 Corinthians 6:9-10*

This verse was written by the Apostle Paul, who also declared the famous phrase:

"For with the heart man believeth unto righteousness; and with the mouth confession is made unto salvation."
    Romans 10:10

The gospel that the apostles preached drove people into substantial changes in their life; not in an hypothetic way, or in a theological position, but in a genuine practice of the holiness Jesus bought for us on the cross.

The primitive church grew in the fear of God and His justice. They honored what Jesus did for them living in such a way that Jesus was glorified.

And they continued steadfastly in the apostles' doctrine and fellowship, and in breaking of bread, and in prayers. And fear came upon every soul: and many wonders and signs were done by the apostles.   Acts 2:42 - 43

It was clear for them that one could not live in the flesh along with the Spirit, as it happens today. Paul makes a clear distinction as a basic part of the Apostles' doctrine:

For what the law could not do, in that it was weak through the flesh, God sending his own Son in the likeness of sinful flesh, and for sin, condemned sin in the flesh: That the righteousness of the law might be fulfilled in us, who walk not after the flesh, but after the spirit.

Romans 8:3 - 4

A genuine conversion transfers the believer into a life in the Spirit. Note how in the passages of Romans, that I already mentioned, God's justice is accomplished when the believer leaves the carnal way of living and turns to listen to the Holy Spirit in order to follow him. When God truly enters the life of someone, they suffer a radical change. Christ living inside of us is a spiritual reality that shakes us from the inside and breaks all of our worldly and sinful schemes. He takes our heart with a powerful strength and immerses us in his gleaming light.

This experience renews our mind. Now we will be thirsty and hungry for the things in heaven. This world will not seduce us anymore. Jesus's seed in us is full of strength, fire, and resurrection. It is GOD LIVING IN US.

But ye are not in the flesh, but in the Spirit, if so be that the Spirit of God dwell in you. Now if any man have not the Spirit of Christ, he is none of His.   *Romans 8:9*

What the apostle Paul is saying here is that the evidence the Holy Spirit dwelling in a person is the fact that he is guided by the Holy Spirit. He has left his sinful way of living and now walks led by the Spirit of Christ.

For as many as are led by the Spirit of God, they are the sons of God.   *Romans 8:14*

Being guided by God means to hear His voice in our conscience, through his Word, even in our dreams or the prophetic words He might speak to us. It is having the "fear of God" as a safe anchor through which the Holy Spirit keeps us in His commandments and paths.

The powerful gospel of Jesus Christ is actually a call to follow Him. It is not a formula or a prayer without compromise. Our salvation settles in our answer towards the sacrifice of Jesus, surrendering our life with a sincere heart in order to be forged by His power.

We will not be saved until we determine to live in Christ. Maybe we are walking towards salvation, but we will not be sealed until we truly put our life on the cross. Some people decide to follow him and give him their life in a radical way. They make a simple prayer that comes from the deepest part of their heart and they are sealed in that very moment. Others get closer to the Lord little by little, until they surrender their hearts totally. Others just pray for repentance before they die and this is enough for God to save them.

The times and the heart of each man are different; there is not a formula, so we cannot put them all in the same bag.

And they that are christ's have crucified the flesh with the affections and lusts.   *Galatians 5:24*

It does not say: "They crucify the flesh little by little", as God deals with their life, as it is taught nowadays.

Salvation not only refers to what it is said in Romans 10-9-10, but it also involves the deep comprehension of the whole New Testament. It is part of a series of truths that compliment each other and give salvation substance.

God is restoring both the way we understand and appreciate salvation, as well as the preaching of His gospel. It is not time anymore to live vituperating against His name with injustices of all kinds. God is restoring the right way to live as His body, so that we may raise up His name by living a holy life and giving Him the honor that He deserves.

6.- There is a difference between being a sinner and an immature Christian.

The Bible considers a sinner the man who practices sin, that is to say, according to the rudiments and passions of this world. The Bible is referring to the one who willingly sins both, by ignoring the sacrifice of Christ not having ever listened about His name, or having knowledge of Him.

None of the apostles who wrote the New Testament

considered someone who lived in sin as "born again" nor "full of the Holy Spirit". The Bible makes a substantial difference between the sinner and immature Christian.

It is one to be carnal and a child in Christ and to say, "I am of Paul"; and another , "I am Apollo 's" (1 Corinthians 3:1-7) and something very different is to be an adulterer , someone who robs , someone who deceives his fellow man, or someone who asks a fortune-teller, and calls himself a believer.

One thing is the lack of a renewed mind in Christ and to feel offended when someone hurts us, and another is to commit fraud or be immersed in pornography through the internet.

Although all sins soil our soul and our spirit, there are sins of death and sins of immaturity.

If any man see his brother sin a sin which is not unto death, he shall ask, and he shall give him life for them that sin not unto death. There is a sin unto death: I do not say that he shall pray for it. All unrighteousness is sin: and there is a sin not unto death. We know that whosoever is born of God sinneth not; but he that is begotten of God keepeth himself, and that wicked one toucheth him not.   *1 John 5:16-18*

There are some theologians that say this passage refers to the blasphemy against the Holy Spirit; nevertheless, in the whole context of this letter, this topic is never mentioned by John. What it is actually abundant in these scriptures, is the deep revelation that he had related to the ones who belong to God and the ones that do not.

Along this whole epistle, the apostle is talking about how important it is to live without sin. This makes me deduce that John refers to all what is called sin in the law of Moses, that is to say, all the sins we already know that are sins.

Remain holy, without practicing the sin of the world, does not mean be legalistic nor "living according to the law". But, "living according to the Spirit" is the consequence of being guided by the Holy Spirit of God.

Jesus said:

Think not that I am come to destroy the law, or the prophets: I am not come to destroy, but to fulfil. For I say unto you, that except your righteousness shall exceed the righteousness of the scribes and Pharisees, ye shall in no case enter into the kingdom of heaven.

Matthew 5:17 and 20

This does not mean someone cannot stumble and eventually fall into failure. The word says well: "we have an advocate in heaven, Jesus Christ the righteous."

I am talking about the fake people who have been years in the church and still love the world and practice sin, believing that they will go to heaven by grace; people who have never experienced a true encounter with the sacrifice of Christ in relation to their own life. They believe they are saved because they repeated a prayer someone made for them.

Going back to the topic, let us see how the apostle Paul makes a difference between a "sinner" and a "carnal or immature Christian." If we read carefully his epistles to the Corinthians, we will realize that there were immature people in the church, there were divisions, competence and jealousy; but there were not practices of sin of death. We can see as a proof of this in the case of a man who was found to commit incest. This case is so remarkable and unusual, that it is worthy to mention as something unprecedented.

But now I have written unto you not to keep company, if any man that is called a brother be a fornicator, or covetous, or an idolator, or a railer, or a drunkard, or an extortioner; with such an one no not to eat. For what have I to do to judge them also that are without? do

not ye judge them that are within? But them that are
without God judgeth. Therefore put away from among
yourselves that wicked person.

1 Corinthians 5:11 and 13

In his second epistle, he writes with a deep sadness
for that man:

But if any have caused grief, he hath not grieved me,
but in part: that I may not overcharge you all. Sufficient
to such a man is this punishment, which was inflicted of
many.   *2 Corinthians 2: 5 - 6*

Note how this was not usual in the church. All of
them were deeply sad because one had committed
sin. Jesus never compromised his principles in order
to have more followers. When the rich young man
comes to Him and asks Him how to enter the kingdom
of God, He answers something that shakes him and
makes him go away.

And, behold, one came and said unto him, Good Master,
what good thing shall I do, that I may have eternal life?
And he said unto him, Why callest thou me good? there
is none good but one, that is, God: but if thou wilt enter
into life, keep the commandments. He saith unto him,
Which? Jesus said, Thou shalt do no murder, Thou shalt
not commit adultery, Thou shalt not steal, Thou shalt not
bear false witness, Honour thy father and thy mother:

and, Thou shalt love thy neighbour as thyself. The young man saith unto him, All these things have I kept from my youth up: what lack I yet? Jesus said unto him, If thou wilt be perfect, go and sell that thou hast, and give to the poor, and thou shalt have treasure in heaven: and come and follow me. But when the young man heard that saying, he went away sorrowful: for he had great possessions.   *Matthew 19: 16 -22*

Jesus did not accommodate the gospel in order to seduce a soul and make a proselyte. He did not even talk to the Pharisees with "evangelistic wisdom" for them to follow Him. Jesus made them see what was in their hearts, so that they might repent and follow him with all their heart.

Nowadays, the rich young man would be told: "Do not worry, if you do not want to give your money (lover, idol, alcohol, hatred, etc.) Jesus already gave his life for you. Let me pray for you and Jesus will come to live in your heart."

Do you really think He will come? SELAH. What are we doing with a gospel that actually has power to save?

God's true love shows us with great mercy what is wrong in us so that we may be reconciled with the Father. Jesus' mission is reconciliation.

We need to see how painful our sin is to the Father in order to understand salvation. Our sin deeply hurts God's heart, and so it does the body and soul of Jesus. We cannot continue preaching a gospel that omits this confrontation.

7. – Called to be a new generation in Christ.

God wants us to deeply understand what being a new creation in Christ means. This is one of the most important foundations of our life, and God is providing us with a fresh light to understand it clearly.

This may be one of the most preached topics in the church, but also one of the less understood. So, open your heart for I want you to receive this powerful truth of a new apostolic reformation:

Therefore if any man be in Christ, he is a new creature: old things are passed away; behold, all things are become new.   *2 Corinthians 5:17*

What is it to be a new creation?

Being a new creation does not mean to be accepted as members of a church, nor changing denominations. It is not changing our behavior or moral habits. It is not stopping attending mundane parties in order to start attending a church. It is not leaving our old friends and having Christian friends. It is not reading the Bible, or taking all of the Christian education classes that we can attend.

All of these actions can be achieved without ever becoming a new creation in Christ. In fact, this is offered by any religious system that includes the name of Jesus. For instance, institutions like the Roman Church, the Jehovah Witnesses, the Mormons, the Light of the World and other kinds of cult pseudo Christian organizations, including the Masons encourage these activities.

Religion is the alternative offered by the devil to make us believe we are fine with God under a veil of piety and appearance but, denying its efficiency. It makes us believe that the external of the letter can replace the essence of the spirit.

This is so subtle that it has deceived millions of Christians apparently "born again". This is why the Spirit stated phrases like:

I know thy works, that thou hast a name that thou livest, and art dead.

Revelation 3:1b

These are spots in your feasts of charity, when they feast with you, feeding themselves without fear: clouds they are without water, carried about of winds; trees whose fruit withereth, without fruit, twice dead, plucked up by the roots;   *Jude 1:12*

The new creation is the resurrection of our spirit. It is not what we may do religiously but what we become. The conversion is not the adoption of a new philosophy but a complete change in the essence of our being. Something new and wonderful will start operating inside of us; something that was not there before and couldn't be done by men.

This is the resurrection of Christ giving our spirit life, in other words, the power of the resurrection working in us. This operation will give birth to a totally different creature, a spiritual one, alive and powerful; one who contains all the glory of the resurrection.

Although the flesh is the structure formed by the principles of a fallen nature, the new creation is the spiritual structure formed by the divine.

How can we become new creatures? First, we must understand that the spirit of the natural man is dead because of sin.

"The payment of sin is death". This means our spirit lacks God's life. This death is the separation between God and men. In a huge portion of the human being, the spirit remains in a lethargic condition; it is asleep without the slightest interaction with the soul in relation to God.

In some other people, their spirits have been awakened by spirits of darkness that activate it in order to use them in occultism, new age, Zen Buddhism, asceticism, mental control, or hallucinogenic drug consumption. That is why people who are involved in such practices have experienced the supernatural.

In counted exceptions God awakens the spirit of someone unconverted, for instance, in the case of Cornelius, who was the first gentile receiving the gospel through the apostle Peter. This also happens to people who, without knowing the Lord, receive revelation from God in their spirit and, eventually, reconcile with God.

The spirit is the most powerful part of men, and the devil knows it very well. That is the reason why he is so interested in activating them in order to control the spiritual world through his followers.

The eternal part of man is his spirit. The soul only adheres to this part to follow it in its final destiny. The soul was created to be the means through which our spirit related with the world, being that the spirit is the one that is to govern our being. After the fall of men, the soul took the authority over our being, and a transference in the personality occurred. The "I" of men stopped being spiritual to become "soulical". We stopped receiving God's life and entered into a death condition where the devil took all the control.

When someone dies, his sleeping spirit or spirit disconnected from God goes back to Him, who gave it. In the meantime, the soul separated and goes to its eternal condemnation.

What it is saved or condemned is the soul. If someone receives Jesus in his spirit and submits his soul to God's government, his soul will be saved and the seat of his personality will be transferred to his spirit again. Whereas, someone who does not receive Jesus will suffer eternal condemnation in his soul. However much alive, the soul feels. However much good it is, it's final destiny depends on the condition of the spirit.

A spirit, who has not been refreshed by the union with Christ, will continue in it's death condition. Jesus Christ is the only one who may reconcile men with God by refreshing their spirit. It is in the spirit, where the bridge between God and men is established. This does not happen at the level of the soul, which lacks of death or life (as the spirit does) by itself. It is just an instrument to keep us in touch with the material and animal world.

Men were created to be a governing SPIRIT. That is its vital essence and that is the only place where they can receive salvation. Salvation and new birth are not achieved via an intellectual mechanics, but it is a matter of the spirit. The spirit must be engendered by the Spirit of God.

But as many as received him, to them gave he power to become the sons of God, even to them that believe on his name: Which were born, not of blood, nor of the will of the flesh, nor of the will of man, but of God.

John 1:12 - 13

It is not the will of the flesh that produces this engenderment, but God awards it. He brings the precious seed of life and plants it in our spirit. This happens when with a sincere and repentent heart we give Him all that we are. Then, we are baptized.

Then Peter said unto them, Repent, and be baptized every one of you in the name of Jesus Christ for the remission of sins, and ye shall receive the gift of the Holy Ghost. Then they that gladly received his word were baptized: and the same day there were added unto them about three thousand souls.   *Acts 2:38 and 41*

In the New Testament, the consummation of the faith people had believed was immediately confirmed by the baptism.

He that believeth and is baptized shall be saved...
                                                        Mark 16:16 a

It is in the baptism where the union of our spirit with God's Holy Spirit takes place, and a new spiritual creature is engendered and starts growing in God's resemblance. God's life in us is in the resurrection. All the power Jesus Christ arose with from death is now what dwells in our spirit.

The baptism is not immersing in the waters in the name of Jesus, but the decision to die to our sinful life in order to be reborn in Him. It is crucifying this world with all its desires and passions, just as Jesus did.

Therefore we are buried with him by baptism into death: that LIKE AS CHRIST was raised up from the dead by the glory of the Father, even so we also should walk in newness of life. For if we have been planted together in the likeness of his death, we shall be also in the likeness of his resurrection: Knowing this, that our old man is crucified with him, that the body of sin might be destroyed, that henceforth we should not serve sin.
                                                        Romans 6:4 - 6

It is very clear that Christ is our model to follow in what baptism actually means; this is why I remark the words: "like as Christ..."

The first design is death, then the resurrection. The baptism is a design of death. If we do not enter the waters with the firm conviction to die in the flesh and sin, then, we just get wet. The water does not have power for salvation, but what it does is represent the decision to die in order to be resurrected. This might be done with all of our heart and conscience.

There are people that enter the waters as a mere religious requirement, but without the genuine conviction to follow Jesus with all their being. Maybe they need to be accepted, want to be part of a group to feel integrated in society, want to please their wife, or vice versa.

Then, this important event becomes an errand, as someone who gets a passport. However, their hearts never truly had a desire to die with Christ.

I know several cases of people who enter the waters so as to conquer the heart of a beautiful girl member of the church, because they feel frustrated in their careers, or unsuccessful in their businesses and want to see if their "luck" changes by trying "Christianity".

There are people who join a church just because they are lazy and want the merciful fellows to solve their problems. Others get baptize because someone from the group encouraged them. Others do so under family pressure. I can name many more examples and cases I have witnessed when ministering to people in different churches.

In all the cases mentioned before, neither the baptism nor the new life took place; it was just a religious ritual. "We are not engendered by the will of the flesh" which is why, when the time has passed by, we do not see changes or fruit in these people. That is why we see so much indifference in the church. People consider the prayers boring. They do not know what to say to evangelize and when they hear the word tithe, they look for lots of excuses not to do it.

The new creation is real, affects our whole being, invades our mind, and destroys the body of sin. It is a visible light and power of God. It is evangelized by nature. It is full of life and fire, because it is God himself united with us.

The new life is just like Jesus died and was resurrected. Jesus suffered a powerful transformation in the grave, in such a way that the one who arose from it was totally different from the one who entered in that cave. Not even the disciples recognized him.

Paul refers to the apostles saying:

Wherefore henceforth know we no man after the flesh: yea, though we have known Christ after the flesh, yet now henceforth know we him no more.

2 Corinthians 5:16

The new creation is not a manifestation in the flesh, but in our spirit, which is transformed by the resurrection.

Once the spirit is engendered, an internal growing begins. Each part of our spirit is awakened and developed. We are more sensitive to the things of the spirit. We begin hating things we used to love, and feel foreign to mundane environments. It bothers us to listen to rude words and, above all, we hate sinning and making the Holy Spirit sad.

The new creation longs for the things from above. It cannot remain silent. It has to tell everybody about Jesus. It is pleased with praying and giving. It is brave and loves justice. It fears God and loves people. It considered everything else worthless. It lives to win Christ and the power of resurrection, as the apostle Paul said.

Resurrection is not only the final condition of the sons of God, when we were arisen among the dead; it is the power that gives life to the new creation that is being engendered inside of us.

And so it is written, the first man Adam was made a living soul; the last Adam was made a quickening spirit.

1 Corinthians 15:45

The Spirit of Christ engenders our spirit. That which was dead is suddenly filled with life and it is awakened to a spiritual reality that it did not know. All that it longs for is what matters to God. This is not something hypothetic; this new life must be manifested. However, this is not the experience of all the ones who say "Lord, Lord!"

It is because of iniquity that the spirit of millions of persons in the church, still sleeps. For this very same reason many people feel as if they have anchors that prevent them from taking firm steps towards God. Their eyes are bandaged not to see the splendor of the gospel of the glory of Jesus Christ and truly turn to God.

They are satisfied, or maybe self-scarified? NOT SURE OF MEANING in a religious life, but not able to see in their own life the power of God. Some of them know very well what is going wrong and others have no idea.

For this reason this book may be the most important thing you have ever held in your hands. By studying it, you will see and identify this terrible scum that has covered everyone, a scum that God wants to remove once and for all from our life.

In the last chapter I explained how to get rid of it and how to start enjoying in a genuine way all the Richness of the Glory of God that comes after being engendered by His spirit.

Conclusion

How do we deal with Iniquity?

As we have seen throughout this book, iniquity is not a simple sin that we just ask for forgiveness and end the problem. Iniquity is an entire body of sin and evil, rooted within our spirit. Iniquity has corrupted the whole structure of our thoughts and our behavior, and it has also infiltrated our bones and organs.

Uprooting it takes time and dedication, but it will be the best investment of our lives. The fruit of righteousness, together with the promises and the long-awaited blessings of God will manifest in us. A new chapter awaits, full of great joy and victory in Christ Jesus.

The first thing we must do is ask the Holy Spirit to help us in this wonderful process of deliverance. We must ask him to send us a true spirit of repentance and the courage to change.

Now, pray this prayer with me or pray your own with sincerity:

"Holy Spirit, I come to you today, humbling my heart, asking for a true spirit of repentance to come over me. Open my spiritual eyes so that I can see my iniquity. Give me your gifts of revelation, dreams and words of knowledge, so that I can understand what my ancestors did, that is affecting my life, bringing curses and obstacles that hinder me from living the life of abundance and the blessings of Your Kingdom."

What you must do next is consecrate the moment of your conception. In the Kingdom of God and in the invisible world there is no time or reason why we cannot amend some things according to God's will. Imagine your father's small sperm and your mother's ovule that gave you life. Now, pray something like this:

"Heavenly father, in this moment I consecrate the sperm of my father who gave me life, and declare it clean by the blood of Jesus Christ,

therefore, holy and perfect. I declare that it becomes full of Your Spirit and your life. I also consecrate my mother's ovule and declare it clean by the blood of Jesus Christ and full of your life. I consecrate to Your Holy name Jehovah, the Almighty God, the very moment of my conception. I declare it blessed, full of your eternal purpose, covered by Your blood and hand. I declare my life will accomplish all that I was created for. I surrender my life to you from this moment on and receive Your DNA with all of the spiritual inheritance that there is in Your blood. In the name of Jesus, amen."

Now, take a notebook in which to jot down everything that the Lord brings to your remembrance or shows you. Review the list provided in the Bible as being iniquity. Pray over each of these sins, one at a time. Take a moment as you go over the list, waiting for the Spirit to bring conviction, memories or revelation. Then, confess your iniquity and the iniquity of your ancestors. It is likely that you have committed the same sins that they committed, since this is recorded in your spiritual inheritance.

Let's begin in Isaiah 59, the chapter of iniquity by excellence:

But your iniquities have separated between you and your

God, and your sins have hid his face from you, that he will not hear. For your hands are defiled with blood, and your fingers with iniquity; your lips have spoken lies, your tongue hath muttered perverseness. None calleth for justice, nor any pleadeth for truth: they trust in vanity, and speak lies; they conceive mischief, and bring forth iniquity. Lying tongues: Religiosity, pagan religious practices, hypocrisy, and all kinds of fraud or deceit.

Isaiah 59:2-4

A wicked tongue: Slander, gossip, cussing, sarcasm, poisonous tongue, bearing false witness, and murmuring.

Not crying out for justice: Lack of compassion in the face of other's misfortune, indifference to the sins of cities, and indifference to the sin of the church. We have the ability to do well, but don't do it.

Not judging with truth: Making judgments in a hurry, showing favoritism to those we love or those who profit us, showing favoritism to the rich over the poor and racism.

Trusting in vanity and speaking vanity: Trusting in riches, trusting in the system of this world, putting our trust in man, medicine, our salary, or the insurance of this world and talking about it.

Thoughts of iniquity: Revenge, plotting evil, boycotting the work of God, all of the thoughts in which we plan to do evil to someone else, and resentment and bitterness.

Not walking in righteousness, via twisted paths: Trusting in our own righteousness instead of God's, taking the lordship of our life, putting our decisions above those of God, any road that does not lead us to righteousness, twisting the will and peace of God, not keeping a commitment, vow or promise, and causing others to suffer.

Rebellion before God and His statutes.

Departing from following God: Following and trusting other gods, idolatry, occultism, witchcraft, divination, new age, satanism, spiritualism, and sectarianism.

This is the list found in the 10 commandments. Exodus 20:1–17 (excluding those already mentioned).

Taking the name of God in vain: swearing by His name, using it without respect as expressive exclamations, telling jokes using His name and blaspheming.

Not resting: (although the now-Jewish Christian

does not need to keep the Sabbath) Resting in God is a way for Christians to trust Him. In addition, not resting our bodies breaks a natural law of life. Stress and anxiety are iniquitous.

Not honoring your father and mother: lack of respect for authority, speaking poorly about them, and not treating them with dignity and love.

Committing adultery: Fornication, pornography, sexual perversion, unnatural, inappropriate use of the body or your spouse, all kinds of sexual aberration, uncleanness, lasciviousness, orgies, impurity, unruly **passions, and incest.**

Stealing: Fraud, changing property boundaries with the intention of robbing, falsifying measures, paying unjust salaries, and tax evasion.

Coveting: your neighbor's spouse, his servants or his goods and the things of this world.

This is the list in Galatians 5 (excluding those already mentioned).

Strife: Verbal or physical violence, enmity, arguing, jealousy, bad temper, dissentions, anger, sowing discord, and divisions.

Heresy: Changing the context of the Word, twisting Scripture in order to control and dominate people by intimidating them, using the Word to obtain dishonest gain, and interpreting the Word in order to justify sin or lack of integrity.

Drunkenness: Addiction to any drug, smoking.

Envy: Wicked desires.

This is the list of Colossians 3 (excluding those already mentioned).

Greed: Trusting in riches, indifferent to the needs of the poor or the work of God, and idolatry of goods of this world (to possessions that can be "touched").

Love of the world.

Disobedience: To God, to His Word, and to authority; lack of submission; and having a rebellious and independent spirit.

This is the list in 2 Timothy 3 (excluding those already mentioned).

Love of oneself, despotism, Loving "I", vanity, pride, haughtiness, and tyranny; bragging, considering yourself superior to others and conceit.

Ungrateful: Feeling we are the owners of what we possess,without realizing that everything belongs to God and not living gratefully and according to what Jesus did for us.

Lack of natural affection: Selfishness.

Discontent: Never content and never satisfied with the blessings of God.

Intemperate.

Merciless.

Cruelty: Sadistic, masochistic; and mental and verbal cruelty.

Treason: Disloyalty.

Loving pleasure more than God.

Corruption: Conspiracy.

This is a list of other sins:

Eating blood or drown animals and eating cured meats made with blood or eating animals that have not been drained of blood.

Tempting God: Criticizing God or accusing Him.

Eating what has been sacrificed to idols, and participating in pagan festivals in which food dedicated to idols is eaten, such as festivals for the dead, Halloween, saints or virgins.

Profaning what is holy: Profaning our bodies, tattoos, or body piercing.

Prostitution: Selling oneself for money and selling principles for riches.

Divorce. (Those not justified by fornication or mistreatment).

Homosexuality: Bisexuality.

Sexual depravation: Bestiality (sex with animals), pedophilia (sex with children), and necrophilia (sex with dead).

Unbelief: Distrustful hearts, double-minded, pessimism, and fault finding.

Fear: Lack of Faith.

Forgetting the poor and the widows.

No fear of God.

Usury: Lending money with interest or taking advantage of those who have borrowed money.

I have tried to make this list as extensive as possible in order to provide better tools for your liberation. To me, there is nothing more wonderful than solving a mystery, and discovering what has been hindering my walk with God, and then removing it.

As I have advised in previous chapters, at times it will be necessary to make detailed, exhaustive lists. This is not really a requirement for your salvation; it is for your total liberty and blessing. Once you have asked forgiveness very specifically in each area that you have identified with; command all iniquity to be uprooted from your spirit and soul.

Then, command the physical substance produced by the iniquity to be loosened from your bones and organs, and command it to exit your body. As these are literal liquids, they will leave the body through diarrhea, vomiting, excessive urine, phlegm and runny nose as if one had a cold. All this is perfectly natural and will leave in this way.

It is a good idea when you are commanding these substances to exit your body, that you touch all of your joints and place your hands on the different body parts. If someone full of the Holy Spirit can help you, tell him to place his hands on each joint of the vertebrae in your back while you command the iniquity to leave.

You can pray something like this:

Lord, I ask you to forgive my iniquity and the iniquity of all of my ancestors. We have all sinned against you. But today I repent for my entire ancestral line because we have committed...[name the specific sins]. I ask you to forgive us and to cleanse me. Purge from my spirit, soul and body all of these iniquities.

I command all iniquity residing in my bones and in my organs to leave my body right now. Iniquity, leave my bones and my organs in the name of Jesus!

Continue doing this until it manifests and it is out. It may take hours or even days for all of it to leave. You may feel a little tired, but this is totally normal. You will recover quickly.

Once you have done this, cancel the curses that

have resulted from the iniquity in your life. Now you are ready for the righteousness of God to be established upon your life, and all of the blessings of God.

Final Prayer

My Final Prayer for you:

Father, I ask you, according to your mercy, righteousness and truth, to establish my brother (sister) in Your divine righteousness. From this day on, he (she) will be established as righteous, first of all by your selfless sacrifice, and secondly, because he (she) has departed from iniquity to follow your kingdom. I declare upon him (her) that all your blessings and your goodness will come upon him (her) and will overtake him (her). I declare that your mercy will rest upon his (her) generations.

So shall they fear the name of the LORD from the west, and his glory from the rising of the sun. When the enemy shall come in like a flood, the Spirit of the LORD shall lift up a standard against him. And the Redeemer shall come to Zion, and unto them that turn from transgression in Jacob, saith the LORD. As for me, this is my covenant with them, saith the LORD; My spirit that is upon thee, and my words which I have put in thy mouth, shall not depart out of thy mouth, nor out of the mouth of thy seed, nor out of the mouth of thy seed's seed, saith the LORD, from henceforth and for ever.

Isaiah 59:19-21

Bibliography

[1] Méndez Ferrell, Ana *"Regions of Captivity,"* Voice of The Light Ministries, 2009.

[2] Méndez Ferrell, Ana *"The Dark Secret of G.A.O.T.U,"* Ana Méndez Ferrell, Inc. 2011.

[3] Eckhardt, John *"Identifying and Breaking Curses,"* Whitaker House, 1999, pg. 12.

[4] Méndez Ferrell, Ana *"Seated in Heavenly Places,"* New Edition enlarged and increased Voice of The Light Ministries. 2010.

[5] Watchman, Nee *"The Spiritual Man,"* Christian Fellowship Publishers, Inc, 1968. Reprinted as a combined edition in 1977.

[6] Ibid.

Visit our new website

www.voiceofthelight.com

Write to:
Voice of The Light Ministries
P. O. Box 3418
Ponte Vedra, FL 32004
USA

Email us on our website:
http://voiceofthelight.com/contact-us/

Follow us on **FACEBOOK & TWITTER**
Watch us on **Frequencies of Glory TV & YOUTUBE**

www.frequenciesofglorytv.com

www.youtube.com/user/VoiceoftheLight

www.facebook.com/AnaMendezFerrellPaginaOficial

www.twitter.com/AnaMendezF

CPSIA information can be obtained
at www.ICGtesting.com
Printed in the USA
LVHW022136080520
655244LV00002B/547